CAMBRIDGE MUSIC HANDBOOKS

Haydn: String Quartets, Op. 50

CAMBRIDGE MUSIC HANDBOOKS

GENERAL EDITOR Julian Rushton

Cambridge Music Handbooks provide accessible introductions to major musical works, written by the most informed commentators in the field.

With the concert-goer, performer and student in mind, the books present essential information on the historical and musical context, the composition, and the performance and reception history of each work, or group of works, as well as critical discussion of the music.

Other published titles

Bach: Mass in B Minor   JOHN BUTT
Beethoven: *Missa solemnis*   WILLIAM DRABKIN
Berg: Violin Concerto   ANTHONY POPLE
Handel: *Messiah*   DONALD BURROWS
Haydn: *The Creation*   NICHOLAS TEMPERLEY
Janáček: *Glagolitic Mass*   PAUL WINGFIELD
Mahler: Symphony No. 3   PETER FRANKLIN

Haydn: String Quartets, Op. 50

W. Dean Sutcliffe
St Catharine's College
Cambridge

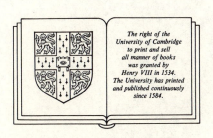

The right of the
University of Cambridge
to print and sell
all manner of books
was granted by
Henry VIII in 1534.
The University has printed
and published continuously
since 1584.

Cambridge University Press
Cambridge
New York   Port Chester
Melbourne   Sydney

Published by the Press Syndicate of the University of Cambridge
The Pitt Building, Trumpington Street, Cambridge CB2 1RP
40 West 20th Street, New York, NY 10011–4211, USA
10 Stamford Road, Oakleigh, Victoria 3166, Australia

© Cambridge University Press 1992

First published 1992

Printed in Great Britain at the University Press, Cambridge

A catalogue record for this book is available from the British Library

Library of Congress cataloguing in publication data
Sutcliffe, W. Dean.
Haydn: String Quartets, Op. 50 / W. Dean Sutcliffe.
p.   cm. – (Cambridge music handbooks)
Includes bibliographical references and index.
ISBN 0 521 39103 2. – ISBN 0 521 39995 5 (pbk)
1. Haydn, Joseph, 1732–1809. Quartets, strings, H. III, 44–9.
I. Title. II. Series.
ML410.H4S83   1992
785′.7194 – dc20   91–14804 CIP MN

ISBN 0 521 39103 2 hardback
ISBN 0 521 39995 5 paperback

Contents

Illustrations

Preface

As with so much of their composer's output, the six string quartets of Op. 50 have suffered simply from being a mere few among the many. Within this genre Haydn arguably wrote more great works in one instrumental form than any other composer; consequently he has fallen victim to his own high standards and productivity. Faced with over forty works of high quality, many of them masterpieces, our natural tendency has been to lean on the last products in the genre. The same is true of most of the forms in which Haydn wrote – the late symphonies and keyboard sonatas, for instance, have also been heavily favoured, both critically and in terms of frequency of performance. This has only so much to do with any inherent superiority over earlier efforts; more relevant here is the implication of the term used to describe the music of this whole period. As James Webster has remarked, the word Classical implies an evolutionary bias, such that each successive group of works must necessarily represent an advance over its predecessors.[1] The last full set of six string quartets, Op. 76, has reaped the benefits of this attitude, while Opp. 20 and 33 have also received much attention, centering on a great musicological debate over which represents the first classically 'mature' set.

Another factor which has also worked against a truly balanced picture of Haydn's output is what is generally referred to as a 'ceaseless experiment-ation' with the shape and form of his works. Haydn's restless, 'experiment-ing' nature has worked against a proper understanding of his earlier music, with the result that his last works are usually regarded as the best, an attitude echoed throughout the literature. It might be preferable to think rather in terms of endlessly new accomplishment, with Haydn's 'experi-mentation' being regarded as a temperamental attribute rather than evi-dence of dissatisfaction with existing works. Had Haydn been able to continue composing through the first decade of the nineteenth century, Op. 76 and the two quartets of Op. 77, for instance, might not be regarded as so canonical, but rather, as just another set of new ideas. Unless we are able to overcome the received notion of ineluctable 'progress' towards a later goal of classical perfection, we are in danger of treating a set such as Op. 50 simply as historical cannon-fodder – by saying, in effect, that today is only significant because it is the day before tomorrow. One welcome consequence of this tendency, and the comparatively slight critical attention Op. 50 has received, however, is that the set may be explored with a fairly fresh ear, both for its value in itself and for its relevance to the composer's wider output. Above all, though, Op. 50 should be seen not as a further stage of 'experimentation' or 'consolidation', but as complete and significant in itself. This is particularly important for a set that contains some of the purest writing Haydn ever accomplished.

If it has not been blessed with an abundance of critical commentary, Op. 50 has nevertheless been fortunate in other ways. Many of the composer's letters relating to the composition and publication of the opus have survived. These give us a vivid insight into Haydn's compositional procedures and his relationship to his publishers, as well as providing a taste of the less than impeccable business practices of the time. Fate has been even kinder to the set in the much more recent past. In 1982 the autograph manuscripts of Nos. 3–6 came to light in extremely unlikely circumstances. Doblinger, who were on the very point of producing a new edition of the works, delayed publication until 1985 so as to incorporate those changes required by the new source, and the resulting miniature scores, DM 735–40, edited by H. C. Robbins Landon, represent the only edition to be recommended. Unfortunately, the quartets have not yet appeared in the *Joseph Haydn Werke* (JHW) collected edition, published by Henle in association with the Joseph Haydn Institute in Cologne. The Dover reprint of the Eulenburg edition, edited by Wilhelm Altmann, has the advantage of cheapness, but it is no critical edition, showing an accumulation of spurious and frequently wrong musical detail that makes for an interesting comparison with the cleaner pages of the Doblinger.

All quartets are referred to here by their customary opus numbers, even though these were assigned by Haydn's publishers rather than by the composer himself. The numbering of the Universal Edition, edited by Christa Landon, is used in references to the piano sonatas, and that of the Doblinger edition, edited by Robbins Landon, for the piano trios. It is ironic that the Hoboken numbering of the symphonies, derived from earlier misleading sources and containing more radical errors of chronology than are to be found in any other genre, has remained unchallenged.

I should like to thank, for their help and for the information they have provided, Dr Georg Feder, Professor H. C. Robbins Landon, and Christopher Hogwood; and, for their patience and advice, Penny Souster and Julian Rushton. Kathryn Bailey, my copy editor, made many valuable suggestions to improve the clarity of the text; I am greatly indebted to her. I am especially grateful to the owners of the autographs of Op. 50 Nos. 3–6, who wish to remain anonymous.

Exact locations in the music are identified in the text through the addition to bar numbers of superscript numbers indicating beats. The Helmholtz system is used to identify pitches (c^1 = middle C).

Origins of the genre

In those times when his music was largely unknown and unplayed (in other words, for most of the nineteenth and at least the first third of this century), Haydn at least retained the distinction of being regarded as the Father of the Symphony and the Father of the String Quartet. While both of these honorifics may now be regarded as untenable from a strict musicological point of view, a quite different type of patriarchy is implied for each genre. Haydn's fatherly role in the development of the symphony consisted simply in the fact that he was an acknowledged leader in the field, the most popular writer in the form, and the one whose works were most in demand. This is apparent from the vast number of spurious works that were marketed under his name during his lifetime in order to increase sales. For the string quartet, however, Haydn's role as head of the family takes on a quite different perspective. Although he did not himself initiate the form of a multi-movement work for four solo stringed instruments without the support of the continuo, Haydn was to play an overwhelming and decisive role in the establishment of the genre. It was he who set the terms for what came to be regarded as the most pure and abstract musical form available to a composer, offering him a chance, so to speak, of writing for himself – and his agents, the four players. The string quartet was subject to few of the constraints that external circumstances could impose upon the composer in other genres: the varying constitution of the eighteenth-century orchestra, the need to keep keyboard sonatas and trios within the stylistic and technical limits of a largely amateur market, or the many and varied limitations set on the composition of sacred music. (For instance, Joseph II decreed that instruments should be allowed to participate in church services only on Sundays and some holidays, a stricture which took effect in the Austrian Empire in 1783.) It was also a largely private form of music-making – no performance of a string quartet in a public concert appears to have taken place in Haydn's lifetime in Vienna.[1] It began to assume a public face only when Haydn sent his six quartets Opp. 54 and 55 to London for performance at the 'professional concerts' in the Hanover Square Rooms.

Such factors combined to lend the quartet several rather conflicting attributes. While it was an intimate and personal form, it also allowed for a more abstract expression of ideas and indeed sometimes took on an academic tinge. If the concerto was the genre in which an instrumental soloist might most fully display his talents, the string quartet was the form in which the composer could most easily display his craft, where social considerations were at their least pressing. While Haydn's example gave the string quartet a prestige as a compositional vehicle that has lasted to some extent to the present day, it also acted as an inhibiting factor on his successors. It took the usually fluent Mozart from 1782 to 1785 to put together a set of six quartets in response to Haydn's Op. 33; the works were dedicated to Haydn and described in the dedication as the 'fruit of a long and laborious effort.' Beethoven did not begin writing his Op. 18 quartets until he was nearing thirty and had already published copiously in the field of chamber music. Brahms waited even longer, not completing his two Op. 51 quartets until 1873 at the age of forty. Furthermore, he had already written then destroyed many complete works.

The elevated status which the string quartet achieved in Haydn's hands stands amusingly at odds with the nature and tone of his first ten quartets, written between about 1757 and 1762. These were called *divertimenti*, and indeed Haydn continued to apply this title intermittently to his quartets until the late 1780s, from which point the term *quartetto* was used exclusively. For the early pieces, however, the title was very fitting, as all ten works are in a five-movement form featuring minuets in second and fourth place. In eight of the quartets a comparatively expansive slow movement occupies third place, while the two others begin with an Adagio (one a set of variations) and feature a scherzo-like Presto as middle movement.

In old editions Haydn is credited with eighteen early string quartets; however, the six works of Op. 3 are not by him, but are possibly the work of a Benedictine monk, Father Romanus Hoffstetter. Of the rest, Op. 1 No. 5 is a symphony (now known as 'Symphony A'), while Op. 2 Nos. 3 and 5 were arrangements of divertimenti for two horns and four strings; in addition there is an E♭ quartet which has been dubbed 'Op. 0'!

This confusion is a product of the proliferation of early editions of Haydn's quartets. The traditional opus numbers no more derive from Haydn than do those of his later works; they first gained wide currency when Haydn's pupil Ignaz Pleyel brought out his collected edition of the quartets, beginning in 1801. For this venture Pleyel drew on the revised form of the edition published in Paris by Louis Balthasar de la Chevardière, which included the Op. 1 No. 5 symphony (the original edition of 1764 representing the first publication of any of Haydn's music). The designation 'Opus I' was garnered from another edition, that of J. J. Hummel in Amsterdam, and Pleyel would have been well advised to have given priority to this edition altogether, for Hummel included 'Op. 0' instead of the misplaced symphony. On the other hand, Pleyel then followed Hummel's 'Opus II' for his collected edition, which contained the two sextet arrangements.

Even this account is a much simplified rendition of the full story, and we are fortunate that modern scholarship has been able to clarify many of the uncertainties surrounding the early quartets. That so many problems await solutions, and that Haydn scholarship has tended to concentrate on the very early music more than is perhaps ideally desirable, has a good deal to do with Haydn's very popularity almost from the start of his career. This popularity guaranteed, as we have seen, that much money was made out of the name of Haydn by publishers, whether the works in question were genuine or not (hence the large number of spurious works which scholars must attempt to authenticate or reattribute). However, not much of this money came Haydn's way. It was some time before the composer realized the true extent of his popularity, which covered Europe to an unprecedented degree, and the realization of the extent of his 'lost earnings' was an important factor in the sharp practice we shall observe in Haydn's dealings over Op. 50.

While the number and publication history of Haydn's early string quartets have now been put in order, the matter of their stylistic origins is still quite unclear. One school of thought has seen in these works a synthesis of several earlier forms and traditions – in particular the *sinfonia* or *concerto à quattro*, where the four string parts were usually meant for orchestral performance with continuo, and the serenade or cassation, involving suite-like forms and possible performance outdoors where the use of harpsichord continuo was impracticable. The *sinfonie* might also on occasion have been played with one instrument to a part, although even then the continuo would generally still have been present, whether indicated or not; and those symphonies with wind parts might also be performed thus simply by omitting those parts, which normally had merely a reinforcing function. (The appearance of the sextets 'Op. 2 Nos. 3 and 5' in this form in Hummel's edition – with incorporation of the horns into the string parts – affirms this practice.)

This, then, was one obvious route to the new genre, although a distinction between orchestral and chamber-musical string parts was immediately observed in Haydn's case: the style of writing in the spurious Op. 1 No. 5 can easily be differentiated from that in the rest of the opus.[2] References to the origins of the form in the serenade have generally been reinforced by evocations of Haydn's own experiences as a young man, when after teaching during the day he would take to the streets at night to perform in a serenading party, in the hope of receiving a gratuity. (For this the word *gassatim* was used, probably cognate with *Gasse*, meaning a narrow street or alley; the alternative label for a serenade, *cassatio*, may also be a development of the term.) The sheer prevalence of this custom seems to have been peculiarly Viennese, with all manner of music being performed, from variations on popular operatic airs to marches and minuets. This very variety must have been what inspired Haydn to the rather Ivesian arrangement related by one of his early biographers, A. C. Dies:

Haydn once took it into his head to invite a number of musicians for an evening serenade [*Nachtmusik*]. The rendezvous was in the Tiefer Graben, where the musicians were to place themselves, some in front of houses and some in corners. There was even a kettledrummer on the high bridge. Most of the players had no idea why they had been summoned, and each had been told to play whatever he wanted. Hardly had this hideous concert begun when the astonished residents of the Tiefer Graben opened their windows and began to scold, to hiss and to whistle at the accursed music from hell. Meanwhile the watchmen, or as they were then called, the *Rumorknechte*, appeared. The players escaped in time, except the kettledrummer and a violinist, both of whom were led away under arrest; however, they were set at liberty after a few days since they could not name the ringleader.[3]

The influence of the serenade can easily be overestimated in a practical, if not in a stylistic sense: it became a vital strand in Haydn's stylistic repertoire, whether found in a fairly direct form (for instance in the second theme of the finale of Symphony No. 71, or Nencio's aria 'Chi s'impaccia di moglie cittadina' from the opera *L'infedeltà delusa*) or more allusively presented, as we shall see in the Adagio of the C major Quartet, Op. 50 No. 2. In practical terms, however, the serenade custom had not exactly sprung up overnight at this opportune time in musical history; the absence of a continuo in this context had not previously opened up the possibility of dispensing with it in other, indoor circumstances. If the serenade or cassation is to be allowed a part in the history specifically of the string quartet, it must be that of a practice that had suddenly become a natural corollary of a rapidly changing musical style. In other words, the role of the continuo in small ensembles had to be already in decline, for reasons that Leonard G. Ratner has elucidated:

In baroque music, the keyboard continuo was the center of the ensemble, governing harmony, rhythm, and sonority. As periodic structure became clarified, harmony grew simpler, with fewer and more regular changes; rhythmic symmetry enabled performers to maintain precision in tempo without the help of the continuo, while the melodic material assigned to leading voices was better projected with a minimum of support, due to its popular style. The sense of the music could be communicated without the support of a continuo.[4]

The danger of overstating the case for these genres as forerunners of or influences on the string quartet lies in an over-reliance on notions of what was 'in the air' at the time as well as a failure to discover more direct compositional models. The second school of thought, which is more influential at the present time, strengthens Haydn's hold on the title of 'father of the string quartet'; Haydn's early quartets are seen to be essentially the logical development of a local tradition confined to Austria, works that are nevertheless almost without exact precedents. Indeed, Haydn's own account of the circumstances that led to his first works in the genre, as related to another biographer, Georg August Griesinger, acknowledges no models:

... the following, purely coincidental circumstance led him to try his hand at the composition of quartets. A Baron Fürnberg had an estate in Weinzierl, several stages from Vienna; and from time to time he invited his parish priest, his estates' manager, Haydn and Albrechtsberger (a brother of the well-known contrapuntist, who played the violoncello) in order to have a little music. Fürnberg asked Haydn to write something that could be played by these four friends of the Art. Haydn, who was then eighteen years old, accepted the proposal, and so originated his first Quartet ... which, immediately upon its appearance, received such uncommon applause as to encourage him to continue in this *genre*.[5]

There was, however, one astonishing anticipation of the genre in the form of Alessandro Scarlatti's four 'Sonate à quattro per due violini, violetta e violoncello senza cembalo', which, although published posthumously in London around 1740, must have been composed some time in the first two decades of the century. For all that these works prefigure materially the new genre, in stylistic terms they are more redolent of the concerto grosso, with its alternations of the ripieno and concertino.[6] In other words, the string parts tend to behave orchestrally. The probability that Haydn was not acquainted with these works does not lessen their historical status, but they exist as isolated specimens that failed to bring forth a creative response – far removed from the impetus provided by Haydn's first ten works to some of his contemporaries.

One of Haydn's own forms that has sometimes been held to prefigure the quartet is the string trio (normally for two violins and a bass), of which he wrote at least thirty-four from the early 1750s until the late 1760s; at this point the quartet once more engaged his attention, and eighteen works (Opp. 9, 17, and 20) were written between 1768 and 1772. However, the differences in his approach to the trio form only serve to increase the sense of fresh beginning apparent in Haydn's account to Griesinger. Most of the trios are in three movements, as opposed to the five of the early quartets, and the arrangement of these three movements also differs; a large proportion are a type of *sonata da chiesa* form, opening with a slow movement, but several other schemes are also used. Thus they do not show the same consistency of approach as the quartets; this is hardly surprising given the longer time-span over which they were composed, but it does indicate that the genre never achieved the immediately distinctive profile of the quartet. A companion piece of negative evidence is that those trios written after 1762 never assume the outer (five-movement) form of the quartet, nor do they move towards the liveliness of ensemble which is one of the factors that must have done most to earn the quartets their immediate popularity. Thus, as far as Haydn is concerned, any suggestion that the quartet was a development or simply a numerical extension of the trio form (for all that the viola frequently doubles the bass line) is untenable.

It is therefore preferable to conceive of Haydn's first quartets as coming into being via the 'suppression' of the thoroughbass,[7] and in a form that shows no precise ancestors. Robbins Landon sums up the situation thus:

Haydn remembered that the quartet originated by accident. Haydn never said that there were not precursors who wrote in four parts for strings in the division of violins I, II, viola and basso (violoncello); but there is no historical evidence that there were any cassatios/divertimenti for that combination before Haydn began to compose his series.[8]

In addition, the quartets inhabited a different stylistic level from those other early works of chamber music, such as the string and keyboard trios – at this time a rather lighter one, with their preponderance of very quick tempi and small-scale metres such as 3/8 and 2/4. Later, the differences in style were to operate in the opposite direction, making the string quartet a typically weightier proposition than its companion instrumental genres.

2

Development of the genre

Three sets of six

It was the best part of a decade before Haydn was able, with Op. 9, to resume the writing of string quartets, and the results differed so radically from the earlier 'cassations' that there seems to be little common ground between the two groups of works. Indeed, near the end of his life Haydn said that he wished his quartets to be remembered as starting with this set from the years 1768–70. By this time Haydn had been in the service of Prince Nicolaus Esterházy for some nine years, and full Capellmeister since 1766. He may therefore have achieved sufficient status and security in his position to be able to undertake an independent venture: in the first instance these quartets were written for himself, and not at the behest of the Prince. Nicolaus constantly demanded new works for the baryton (forming a trio with viola and violoncello), new symphonies, and church music, but none of Haydn's string quartets was to be in any sense commissioned until the 1790s. For all that, Haydn may well have become aware of the enormous success of his early quartets, and the presence of the brilliant leader of the Esterháza orchestra, Luigi Tomasini, would have provided a further incentive to take up the form again. On the other hand, Haydn must also have learnt of the many hostile critical reactions to these early works; as Griesinger informs us, they deplored the 'debasement of music to common fooling' (a complaint that was to be echoed many times throughout Haydn's career). The new tone and technique of Op. 9, however, can hardly be construed as a reaction to such criticism – throughout his career, Haydn was too busy pursuing his own musical ideals to be able to absorb many external models or adverse judgments. In any event, the passing of so much time since the composition of the early works would have guaranteed a new approach in the composer's now greatly enriched style.

The Op. 9 quartets lie near the beginning of the relatively brief period when that style underwent its most complete examination. The years from about 1767 to 1773 yield an extraordinary variety of moods and creative approaches in all genres. The 'Sturm und Drang' label that was often fixed to the products of this period is now largely discredited, implying as it did that all works shared the violence and passion of the 'Farewell' Symphony (No. 45) or the C minor Sonata (No. 33); it is perhaps better to characterize the period as being one of *intensification*, technically, emotionally and formally. Its importance lay simply in the fact that by the early 1770s Haydn had emerged as an indisputably great composer.

Next to the most striking works of their years the Op. 9 quartets appear rather conservative, perhaps with the exception of No. 4 in D minor, which was probably the first to be written. After the brightness and openness of the early ten, they are much more discursive and deliberate, especially in the opening movements. Four of these are marked 'moderato' (or 'allegro moderato') and are in common time, the consequence being detailed rhythmic subdivisions of a slow-moving basic pulse. Haydn had now moved to the four-movement form from which he was not to deviate in his remaining quartets, but he was never, as he did for the symphony, to settle on a decisive order for the inner movements. Here the minuets always occupy second place, presumably in order to avoid the juxtaposition of a relatively slow opening movement with a subsequent Adagio and thus maximize both the internal contrast and the external balance of each work. Thus, now that he had dropped the easy 'framing' construction of the early works, Haydn had constantly to rethink the large-scale proportions of his quartets.

He was also thinking on a still larger scale in this opus, the first, after all, to be designed and composed as a set. This implied giving each work a character of its own, not just in terms of exposing different styles of material and modes of treatment, but, more simply, by setting each in a different tonality. Such deliberate variety of key was by no means the rule in the sets of Haydn's contemporaries. If whole sets were to be balanced by such methods, this implied in turn that the individual work was now to be understood as a whole consisting of four parts rather than as a succession of musical 'numbers', and this indeed represents the most profound change between the early quartets and Op. 9. The achievement of a higher unity, so that one multi-faceted idea seems to rule each work, is not just a matter of material connections between the movements but involves achieving characteristic sonorities and proportions that will only define the behaviour of one particular work. Although the composer can only have reached this ideal to his satisfaction in the Op. 20 set, the first impetus is provided by Op. 9. It would be nice to be able to state that the 'definitive' order in which each opus has come down to us also showed an element of set planning, but, rather less idealistically, it was Haydn's practice to offer his sets 'exclusively' to different publishers in different orders so as to put them off his trail.

The most easily assimilable movements for the present-day listener in both Op. 9 and Op. 17 (written in 1771) tend to be the minuets and finales. As indeed in the composer's earlier works (such as the keyboard sonatas), it is in these movements that Haydn first seems to 'find his feet'; in terms of material, if not of treatment, they are often close to works that lie well in the future (compare, for instance, the C major minuets of Op. 9 No. 1 and Op. 74 No. 1). The trios in particular are consistently impressive, often turning to the minor and allowing Haydn to indulge his epigrammatic tendencies. The trio of Op. 17 No. 1 might be thought of as a companion in technique and mood to the minor minuet of the slightly later 'Trauer' Symphony, No. 44; in calm and inscrutable manner it presents a series of contrapuntal devices at a low dynamic level, with a mysterious retrograde reprise followed by a final shudder to a hemiola rhythm. It is also a model of quartet-writing in a consistently full texture in a medium tessitura (like the more famous slow movement of Op. 20 No. 1). As such it points to another crucial concern of this group of works, the attempt to balance interest more evenly through the four instrumental parts.

The medium could only finally justify its existence by offering rewarding activity to each individual player, there being no public context in which a hierarchy of interest and function would be acceptable. (That this ideal does not amount simply to the so-called equality of all four parts will be discussed further on.) At any rate, Haydn seems to have had his greatest success in achieving the desired flexibility of ensemble in the trios of the present works, perhaps because he is less concerned with melodic exposition as such than with creating a textural and harmonic foil to the minuet. Other significant examples include that in Op. 17 No. 2, which begins by reharmonizing the minuet's closing phrase, but more subtly refers to the equivalent closing phrase of the first half and its two continuations, both back to the start of the movement and on to the second half (see bars 11–13, Example 1). The manner in which it treats these phrases makes the trio somewhat akin to a developmental interlude, giving a strong foretaste of one of Haydn's favourite devices in Op. 50.

The A minor trio of Op. 9 No. 6 again readily achieves textural interest,

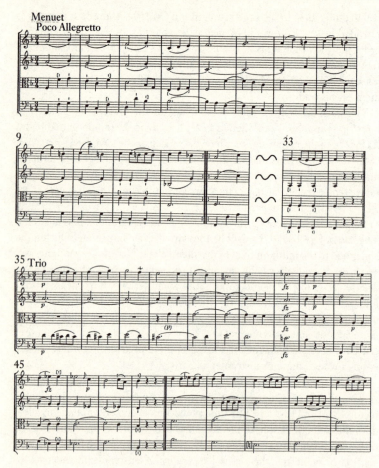

Example 1 Op. 17 No. 2, movement II

but is still more important for its harmonic surprises, first the two perspectives given to the phrase for the upper three instruments first heard at bars 39–42, an early Haydnesque pun, and secondly the manner in which the composer converts the stray Bb heard at the end of the first half into the Neapolitan harmony that colours the end of the second (see Example 2). Such colouristic touches are all the more notable given the comparative lack of harmonic adventure displayed in the two groups as a whole.

Example 2 Op. 9 No. 6, movement II

The finales are typically the most entertaining and successful move-ments in Opp. 9 and 17. Those of Op. 17 Nos. 3 and 6 are perhaps of the highest quality; significantly, they already approximate in spirit, and some-times in the letter, to the fugal finales of the following set, Op. 20. As well as the contrapuntal impulse, both of the Op. 17 movements contain gypsy elements that presage future developments; in addition, bars 39–41 of the No. 6 finale feature a clearing-out of texture and a change of articulation before a major cadence-point that has a very 'high Classical' flavour to it (the conjunction of this feature with the following bars of *bariolage* suggest that Haydn must have had this Presto at the back of his mind when writing the 'Frog' finale to Op. 50 No. 6: compare bars 45–8[1] of that movement with 41–3 of Op. 17 No. 6, shown in Example 3).

What is most significant about the finales from a generic point of view is that a majority of them end quietly, which was hardly an option in the symphony; once again, Op. 17 No. 6 perhaps accomplishes this with the

Example 3 Op. 17 No. 6, movement IV

greatest *éclat*, as the staccato falling third finally falls under one bow, then seems to disappear into thin air.

The greatest problems of appreciation are presented by the slow movements, whose stiff textures have proved to be something of an embarrassment to a later age. Most criticisms of these movements have been based on the lack of 'equality' between the parts, the first violinist acting as a solo soprano to a generally very subordinate accompaniment; one gains the impression that many writers would be more comfortable with a dull movement that was texturally 'sound' than a beautiful one in which the first violin dominates. While the lack of variety in the layout of the parts is a major element in the unsatisfactory effect of these slow movements, a more pertinent fault is that the rhythmic organization is not complex enough to sustain the level of interest typically generated by the faster movements. As Donald Tovey has pointed out, it took Haydn some time to realize that a slow movement cannot merely adopt the rhythmic gestures of a quick movement but at a reduced speed;[1] an instance of such a misplaced gesture can be found in the Adagio of Op. 9 No. 6, where after a beautiful dozen bars the cadence that precedes the recapitulation (at bar 38) contains a distinct 'sag' and invention seems to stop.

The first movements are sometimes unconvincing for similar reasons, given their rather laboured underlying rhythmic sense. With hindsight, and assuredly also from Haydn's point of view in the late 1760s, the language of the early quartets must have seemed over-articulated, where the all-too-frequent cadences dominate instead of being a means to an end. The composer's task in these new works must therefore have been to achieve greater continuity, to make an effort to keep going instead of allowing himself to relax at cadence-points. The effort is very noticeable in the first movements of this period, as can be heard in the comparative frequency of interrupted cadences, substituting a semicolon for the anticipated full-stop

– in later years Haydn is far less reliant on this device. This combination of a certain feeling of strain as well as deliberation is highly uncharacteristic of the composer's work as a whole but is encountered quite frequently in these twelve works. Cornelius G. Burke, in his little-known discography, *The Collector's Haydn*, published in the early days of the recording industry, offers an appreciation of Opp. 9 and 17 that helps to explain why they are not among the composer's more winning works:

Haydn was nearly forty when he composed them, and we can feel him reaching toward a deeper expressiveness in a form still unfixed and docile to who would control it. I do not think he controls it here: the spontaneity of the breezier early works has been compromised by preoccupations with betterment. These quartets are spotted with discontinuous beauties that betray their position of transition between divertimento and sonata: the architect is in conflict with the decorator. Few of the movements ... sustain a deep interest unless we are fascinated by an unparalleled opportunity to hear a man thinking his way to greatness.[2]

The thought and effort invested in these works bore fruit in astonishingly quick time, for Op. 20, completed just a year after Op. 17, occupies a far higher plane; it is characterized above all by a much greater sense of confidence on both emotional and technical levels. Each quartet is utterly individual in its means of expression. No one has been able to explain why such a transformation should have taken place almost overnight, given the length of Haydn's creative career; an inspirational reason might be found in the completion in 1771[3] of the C minor Piano Sonata, No. 33 (the first that Haydn himself called 'Sonata' rather than divertimento or partita). This was probably Haydn's greatest work to date. The unified impulse which sweeps across all of its three movements, allied to a wealth of thematic interconnections, as well as the strength of feeling it communicates must have been a landmark for the composer (so personal, in fact, that Haydn did not have the work published until 1780). There is of course a danger in assuming too much in the way of cross-generic influence, given the natural contrast and different implications of a work conceived for one as opposed to four solo players; Haydn's immediate technical models would have been his previous works in the form, in particular the Op. 17 set. Nevertheless it makes more sense to link these two private forms of music-making than to compare the composer's progress in, say, the quartet and the symphony, which were by now completely distinct modes of thought for Haydn. In many of the symphonies of this time, Haydn was aiming for greater breadth of expression, whereas his goal in the quartets was primarily one of enrichment, of gaining the most from a smaller number of ideas. This same process of intensification is already evident in the C minor Sonata, and some of its spirit has found its way into Op. 20.

Another attribute of the set, one that is rarely dwelt upon, is the heightened sense of colour displayed by the composer. One of the reasons the string quartet has reached its prestigious position in musical life lies in the assumption that it is an ascetic form, drawn in pure lines, restrained black and white, a line-drawing next to the rich oil painting that the orchestra can create. There is a sense of virtue attached to composition in the genre and, indeed, to those who listen to its products. This is really to confuse timbral range with colouristic effect, since the string quartet's intimacy of ensemble can lead to colours and mixtures of equally sensuous effect. For instance, what in an orchestral context might be simply an antiphonal dialogue or exchange between the first and second violin sections becomes in a quartet, once we have properly scaled down our listening, a contrast of tone, inflection and temperament. The greater range of colour in Op. 20 derives partly from a more rigorous application of this very principle (seen simply in the distribution of the main melody through the G major slow movement of No. 3), but also from a stronger feeling for the sheer physical power and effect of musical sound – perhaps the most vivid lesson learnt from Sonata No. 33. This in turn can be seen very simply in the unprecedented eight-part chord that ends the C major Quartet, triple- or quadruple-stopped in every instrument. Even more striking than such demonstrations of force are some of the more delicate effects, such as the trio of No. 6, which is scored literally for three of the instruments, each of which plays exclusively on its lowest string. The minuet of No. 2 dramatically transforms the rhythmic unison gesture of the preceding Capriccio into a calm and warm sonority; on the other hand, the finale of No. 4 features the players as a sort of gypsy band in the liveliest texture imaginable.

How much our perceptions of colour are directed by considerations of texture, register, and spacing can be observed by comparing two extremes of writing. The slow movement of Op. 20 No. 1, as mentioned earlier, maintains a full four-part texture with scarcely a break, the 'glow' of the sound reinforced by packing the lines close together in a medium tessitura. On the other hand, in the Poco adagio of No. 3, from bar 13, the upper three instruments sustain high chords while the cello soliloquizes in its middle and low registers. The same movement also features *bariolage* – the execution of one note on open and stopped strings in alternation – used for accompanimental purposes, a device that is normally confined to quick movements (as in the finale of Op. 17 No. 6). A quite different type of colouring is found in the increased deployment of unisons, whether they are used to punctuate the structure (see the figures at bars 7–8 and 10–11 of the finale of No. 4) or primarily for expressive effect (as in the *fortissimo* declamation at bars 105–6 of the same work's slow movement).

That so many of the outstanding examples of Haydn's widened palette occur in the slow movements is in itself significant: the variety of their textures and forms represents a major advance from Opp. 9 and 17. The older arioso mode is still present, in No. 6, but there the viola shadows and counterpoints the first violin to give greater fluency to the texture; the Un poco adagio e affettuoso of No. 4, on the other hand, forms the first example in Haydn's work of a variation movement placed second in the cycle. The melodic lead in the first variation is shared by second violin and viola, the second is led by the cello, and there is an unusually long and dramatic coda.

The placement of the minuets within the cycle alternates between second (Nos. 1, 3, and 5) and third (Nos. 2, 4, and 6); once more, this is not a matter of 'experimentation' or evidence of a 'transitional' phase. It is simply that Haydn, typically, refuses to make any routine assumptions and orders the inner movements according to the needs of the particular work. Thus in the minor-key Nos. 3 and 5 the slow movements, both in the tonic major, gain an additional sense of repose through following two movements in the tonic minor; on the other hand, the 'Menuet alla Zingarese' of No. 4, in third place, allies itself with the gypsy flavour of the finale.

It is the finales, and in particular those three in fugal style (Nos. 2, 5, and 6), that have claimed most critical attention in discussions of Op. 20; they have all too often been treated as a case apart from the rest of the movements rather than as a quite natural extension of their increased textural flexibility. Paul Griffiths takes issue with the assumption that these fugues are indebted to any dialogue principle: 'op. 20 is an astounding achievement away from the main route of the string quartet's development, most spectacularly and mercilessly bizarre in its fugues, since fugue, in its ordained responses, its direct imitation and its lack of characterization in the voices, is the very antithesis of dialogue ... '[4] This viewpoint is original in the context of much critical opinion in that it isolates the fugues from the rest on textural rather than stylistic grounds; what Griffiths overlooks, however, is that none of the fugues is monothematic. They have two, three, and four subjects in Nos. 5, 6, and 2 respectively, which means that the interchange of material is a more complex and livelier process than one might expect. In addition, Haydn characterizes them further by a *sempre sotto voce* direction, an extreme of dynamic containment that is in each case rudely broken by a loud peroration; this further removes any potential formality by inviting closer detailed listening as it dramatizes the texture. An admirable deconstruction of Op. 20's 'fugue problem' has been provided by David Wyn Jones:

The fugues have often been described as a conscious return to the baroque, as if the classical style were admitting to some stylistic weakness by having a good old-fashioned fugue. But this hopelessly misrepresents the music itself, ignores its context in Haydn's development and in that of contemporary Austrian music in general. Haydn's public would not have regarded a fugue in chamber music as strange or unusual since there was a strong tradition of fugal writing for small ensembles, exemplified by Haydn's predecessor, Werner, and, in the 1760s, in literally dozens of quartet fugues by Gassmann. This is a forgotten, largely sterile repertory to which others, like Ordoñez and Albrechtsberger, were later to contribute, and it contains nothing to rival the spontaneity of Haydn's op. 20 fugues, particularly those in C and A major. This spontaneity had been hard won, the result of a decade of conscious assimilation of contrapuntal procedures. At the same time Haydn was striving, in the quartet genre, to involve all four players in the argument, a process that also culminated in the six quartets of op. 20. Thus the fugues in op. 20 form a natural, unforced conclusion to their respective quartets, testimony to Haydn's unique achievement *c*. 1770, whereby classical homophony could move without any sense of dislocation to polyphony.[5]

If the fugues need not present any problems of comprehension, there is one facet of the works that does not wear well, one which was to remain problematic for some further time in Haydn's output: the use of sequence. An example can be found from bar 50 in the first movement of No. 1; the squareness of harmonic movement is a minor problem, but the rhythmic repetition and textural monotony are something of an anomaly by the terms of Haydn's newly-considered quartet style. The aridity that affects this passage derives from its stylistic misplacement; the lack of flexibility in inflection here is foreign to the Classical style, which is more naturally yielding and rhetorical, and is instead redolent of the 'driven' style of the Baroque. Similar problems can be observed in the first movement of No. 4, which retains some of the laboured rhythmic sense of Opp. 9 and 17: in particular, the hierarchy of accent and stress that the new style was developing is often absent here.

A final, more positive attribute of Op. 20 as a whole is the formal freedom it displays. Almost from the start Haydn showed himself capable in this respect; the difference here is that he is now able to make this liberty serve expressive purposes. An example is the first movement of the G minor Quartet, No. 3, in which the development section does a good deal of recapitulating (in thematic but not harmonic terms), thus leaving the reprise free completely to reshape, rather than restate, the opening argument. The theme then disintegrates at the end, melting into a sustained chord before one last defiant flourish.

The expressive virtuosity of this movement is emblematic of the range inhabited by the whole set – very complex and restless in mood, like the first movement of the C minor Sonata, it moves uneasily between vehemence (the opening theme), irony (the little unison figure that colours the whole movement), bravura (the clarion call first heard at bars 65–6) and even the neurotic hesitancy of the *sopra una corda* figuration. Two other facets of this work are prophetic of concerns that will be central to the examination of Op. 50. The first is the clear gestural connection that obtains between the flourish heard near the end of the first movement and the transitional scale in the first violin at bars 32–3 of the minuet (marked *con forza*, corresponding to the *fortiss.* of the precedent); this is not so much a thematic link, in spite of the identity of pitch and near rhythmic correspondence, as an impulse common to two movements (see Example 4).

The second aspect shows the capacity of Haydn's ear to absorb a strong early dissonance and make it central to the larger progress of a movement. In the minuet the clash of F♯ and F♮ in bar 4 sets the bitter tone of the movement, the melodic F♮ being affectingly reharmonized at the end of the first period; and its force is so strong that its recollection in the coda prompts an extraordinary harmonic turn. The renewed insistence on this semitonal clash causes the minuet to close, not with an apparent *tierce de Picardie*, but, as only Hans Keller seems to have noticed, in the dominant of the subdominant, C minor, an example of 'progressive tonality' across the course of the movement.[6] This in turn has large-scale structural ramifications; the end of the trio rehearses the same dissonance that we are about to hear again upon repetition of the minuet, and it also features at the end of the finale, where the *tierce de Picardie* must be understood not as a 'happy end' but as evidence of exhaustion at the end of a highly complicated work.

The 'New and Special Way'

The Op. 33 quartets, finished in 1781 after a gap of nearly a decade, have been, together with Op. 20, subject to more intensive investigation than any other set of Haydn quartets. This scrutiny was prompted by the

I/259

II/26

Example 4 Op. 20 No. 3

now-famous letter that Haydn circulated to possible patrons offering them manuscript copies of the works prior to publication. Three copies of the letter have survived, and that sent to the Swiss writer J. C. Lavater in Zürich reads:

Most learned Sir and
Dearest Friend!

I love and happily read your works. As one reads, hears and relates, I am not without adroitness myself, since my name (as it were) is known and highly appreciated in every country. Therefore I take the liberty of asking you to do a small favour for me. Since I know that there are in Zürch [*sic*] and Winterthur many gentlemen amateurs and great connoisseurs and patrons of music, I shall not conceal from you the fact that I am issuing, by subscription, for the price of 6 ducats, a work, consisting of 6 Quartets for 2 violins, viola and violoncello *concertante*, correctly copied, and WRITTEN IN A NEW AND SPECIAL WAY (FOR I HAVEN'T COMPOSED ANY FOR 10 YEARS). I did not want to fail to offer these to the great patrons of music and the amateur gentlemen. Subscribers who live abroad will receive them before I print the works. Please don't take it amiss that I bother you with this request; if I should be fortunate enough to receive an answer containing your approval, I would most appreciate it . . .[7]

The emphatic 'new and special way' has received varied interpretations: one camp sees it principally as a mercantile slogan, the other takes Haydn at his word and finds in these works a new perfection and maturity of the Viennese Classical style. The former group has therefore fixed upon Op. 20 as more deserving of 'special' and pivotal status in the composer's wider output, while both opuses have been ransacked for clues in order to establish priority for one of the sets. There is, however, no problem in accepting both senses of the phrase. If Haydn's musical technique had advanced in the intervening nine years, then so had his business acumen; he was becoming an accomplished marketer of his own wares and operator in the murky waters of music publication. He would also have become aware of the generally increased cultivation of the medium, as his letter to Lavater makes clear, although it was particularly strong in Vienna; such composers as Gyrowetz, Ordoñez, Dittersdorf, Vanhal, and Pleyel were both helping to shape and responding to the demand for quartets. On the other hand, Haydn hardly needed the best part of a decade to come up with new ideas; while the 'new and special way' may have been an attempt to re-establish his pre-eminence and market-leadership in this form, it could also stand as a motto for most of what the composer wrote.

Perhaps the main difference between this set and Op. 20 is a rhythmic one. In the interim the composition and production of opera for Prince Nicolaus Esterházy had become Haydn's principal concern, with a regular season having been established in 1776. The demands of operatic composition, including the ability to organize and provide coherence to long stretches of music and the need to vary the pacing of musical events, leave their mark on Op. 33 in its more fluent rhythmic sense. Haydn is more disposed toward repetition of small- and medium-sized units, since he is now thinking on a larger scale – of the cumulative effect of paragraphs, sections, and whole movements. This can be seen most obviously in the finales: three are rondos, and two others are variation movements with strong rondo elements. Concomitant with this is the fact that Op. 33 tends to be simply faster than the earlier sets. This trait is most evident in the substitution of scherzos for minuets (their middle sections are left unnamed). The result, and indeed also the cause, of these characteristics, is what Julian Rushton has described as 'an athletic coordination and economy unique until Beethoven',[8] as Haydn shows a new delight in sustaining his movements by the merest of means.

If enrichment was the password to Op. 20, the goal of its successor seems to be to limit the discussion to a select few topics: less is more. Thus

Example 5 Op. 20 No. 1, movement I

textures become more integrated as the relationship between theme and accompaniment becomes more fluid. Charles Rosen illustrates this point with a negative example from the first movement of Op. 20 No. 1, citing the cello's figure in bar 4, which 'has a purely transitional function, and is never needed except in this place'.[9] This is slightly mischievous, since the figure is a logical inversion of the descending octave arpeggio outlined by violin I in the first two bars – more so, since the shape is clearly echoed in the cello's transitional flourish at bars 29–30 (which is then treated in the developmental sequence discussed earlier). However, Rosen is right to pinpoint the awkwardness here, although it is really a purely rhythmic fault – it is the sextuplet rhythm that, as well as being awkward locally, remains unintegrated into the body of the movement (see Example 5).

Paradoxically, in spite of all these economy measures, the results are characteristically more relaxed than in Op. 20. At the same time an enrichment does take place – in dramatic terms, with 'drama' to be understood as implying not personal expressiveness but a firmer control of the way in which the music moves. This is evident in the first movements of Nos. 1 and 3, with their large-scale exploration of harmonic ambiguities. The value of having a good edition is apparent if one examines the start of Op. 33 No. 1 in the Henle edition – the traditional double-stopping in the second violin is inauthentic, and the single line that replaces it is both more ambiguous and more logical. Haydn suggests a false opening in D major without needing to use a note that is foreign to B minor.

Another paradox is that greater internal contrasts become possible, whether within a movement or an individual work; the first movement of No. 5 includes a respectable textbook second subject, while the concluding rondos of Nos. 3 and 4 feature self-contained gypsy episodes. Friedrich Blume, in his article of 1932 on Haydn's artistic personality as revealed by the quartets, considers that the reincorporation of such opposing impulses constitutes the fundamental intention of Op. 33. For him, the extremes of developmental technique in pursuit of one overriding 'idea' reached in Op. 20 would allow no continuation – a stage Beethoven was to reach only in his late works, while the earlier ones actually lean on late Haydn. Thus the long pause between the composition of the two groups was no coincidence, but is psychologically justified; the danger of 'overheating' in the earlier set is overcome by the greater control of Op. 33. The developmental process is now angled less towards intensification and more towards the formation of conflict, as is apparent from the set's sharper formal boundaries. Blume concludes that Op. 33 is not so much the final consequence of a basic unifying principle as a U-turn from its implications.[10] These lofty thoughts from the bicentenary year of Haydn's birth demonstrate a fundamental truth when one attempts to review Haydn's mature quartet output: his comprehensiveness of mood and technique is so complete that any one opus will yield sufficient evidence to maintain an exclusive point of view. Thus, while Op. 33 represents the major radical step for Blume, Paul Griffiths, as mentioned earlier, imputes the radical intention to Op. 20; the composer's rather inscrutable persona allows a variety of interpretations to compete for the final word about each set. The same richness of views will be seen in the reception history of Op. 50.

The new clarity of the 1781 set has also been given a more social perspective by David P. Schroeder, for whom it marks 'an arrival of refinement and comprehensibility':[11] '[Haydn's] extraordinary achievement was to devise procedures for instrumental music that would allow it an intelligibility previously thought possible only if words were present'.[12] This suggests a different sort of operatic influence on the quartets, aside from those technical considerations previously mentioned: that Haydn might have been trying to introduce a sense of plot to his instrumental work, the *dramatis personae* being those various thematic characters introduced at the start of the action. We are now expected to recognize them immediately they reappear and to be able to follow their interaction. This new narrative and dramatic sense was facilitated by what Charles Rosen has called 'the imitation of speech rhythms in all of Haydn's chamber music' which 'enhance[s] the air of conversation'.[13] Schroeder places this in context by reminding us that the string quartet was the ideal form to be presented at small social gatherings, where intimate and lively conversation would naturally ensue. It is worth remembering that in late eighteenth-century Vienna concerts of all types occupied a quite different status than they do in the present day, when the term 'concert' implies a self-contained musical event. At that time a concert always took place in a wider social context, and that implied a good deal of sociable behaviour, with listeners either talking around or talking through the music. Given the appeal of the string quartet to 'gentlemen amateurs' and 'connoisseurs', however, one may assume that conversation gave way during the performance, which after all in Haydn's case had come to represent a sort of stylized conversation. This yields a further dramatic layer in the 'new and special' form, in that the characters are not just the thematic entities, but also the four players themselves. Schroeder extends this implication from the dramatic to a philosophical realm (one which is underscored by the existence and nature of Haydn's letter to Lavater):

In the string quartets, and in a heightened way with Op. 33, the music places four intelligent people in a 'harmonious' setting, sharing both intellectual and heartfelt experience. The ability to share and exchange the important material offers a strong sense of unified purpose, one in which the player is both aware of his individual importance and the role he plays in creating the whole. In a very real way, then, the quartet became a realization of one of the highest goals of the Enlightenment. With accompaniments that can be transformed to melodies and vice versa, there is an apparent recognition of a higher social truth which is that differences do not preclude equality.[14]

If this suggests a slightly prescriptive and earnest composer, Schroeder corrects the image with reference to the 'conscious shift of language' exemplified by the finale of Op. 33 No. 1:

The theme which begins the movement gives the sense of belonging to an earlier generation. This effect is very much enhanced beginning at bar 13 and lasting until bar 30 where the figuration in the first violin appears to be a parody of Vivaldi or one of his contemporaries ... After a transitional passage (bars 31–42), Haydn introduces material which has a highly comic spirit ... , and appears to snub the preceding material in the earlier eighteenth-century style. At this point, the composer seems to be drawing a line between the old and the new, and by dismissing the old he clearly aligns himself with that which is modern.[15]

This taste for undercutting his own creative work had by now become an important part of Haydn's persona, and one finds this withdrawal into irony or comedy in many future quartets (for instance in the facetious phrase which immediately precedes the reprise in the finale of Op. 64 No. 1, bars 70–2, following as it does a stretch of intricate counterpoint). The tendency is most significant in the present context in that it presents a direct counterpart to an important conversational technique – the withdrawal by means of self-deprecation if one's contribution has become too serious or heated. Perhaps this is why Haydn's stock has always tended to be higher in England than anywhere else. Unfortunately, no such subtext can be found to rescue the sequence in the first movement of Op. 33 No. 4 (at bars 36–47); it is a stylistic blot on the movement and perhaps one of the principal grounds for Hans Keller's refusal to grant the work a place in his book *The Great Haydn Quartets*.[16]

Op. 33 in fact contains a far more pungent example of Schroeder's clash of styles, although it only occurs in the last bar of a movement – the G minor Largo e cantabile from Op. 33 No. 5. The 'new' is represented by a single pizzicato G on all four instruments and is the most extreme instance of ironic deflection in all the composer's output. Indeed, irony may be too gentle a word for the effect of all players twanging an open string after the grave mood of the whole movement and in particular its solemn rhetorical peroration: the movement, it appears, is being cruelly consigned to the rubbish bin. Having poured out his heart, so to speak, the composer now pokes out his tongue. The preceding material is not just old-fashioned in textural terms, but adopts a deliberately archaic style: it is a Baroque aria. One wonders what the 'connoisseurs' of the time made of this gesture. Perhaps they were as embarrassed or disturbed as most modern commentators, of whom an astonishing number have simply avoided the subject. Performers, too, seem to shift uneasily in their seats: the final sound is invariably discreetly produced, which is indefensible in view of the detailed dynamic markings. Haydn would certainly have taken the time to mark *piano* had he required it; as it stands, the *forte* marking of the penultimate bar must be continued to the end. Haydn thus bids an unsentimental farewell not just to this particular movement (he had done the same by means of *col legno* at the end of the slow movement of Symphony No. 67, written in 1778) but to this style and texture for his string quartets altogether. It is significant that Op. 33 No. 5 was probably the first of the set to be written, and that the heavy regularity of its slow movement is succeeded by the most asymmetrical of scherzo themes. This stylistic juxtaposition, and that in Op. 33 No. 1, suggest that Haydn, in a quite unprecedented manner for his time, was using pastiche in order to define his new goals: the claim to a 'new and special way' in the writing of these quartets is argued and won within the context of the works themselves.

3

Capellmeister at Esterháza

That Haydn was able to turn his attention once more to the composition of string quartets was not a little due to the new role that had evolved for him at Esterháza. It has been mentioned that from 1776 there was an annual operatic season, one which grew longer by the year; at the same time, Prince Nicolaus's demand for symphonies and baryton trios was dwindling. For over ten years Haydn's principal task was to be the direction of Italian opera, which involved not just conducting all rehearsals and performances, but also coaching the singers and seeing that all the performance material was in order and appropriate to existing conditions. Where this was not the case, transpositions or rescorings would be required; Haydn would often also delete or add material. Thus, apart from making numerous cuts to quicken the pace of the action (involving an exercise of dramatic judgment that Haydn seemed better able to apply to instrumental works such as Op. 33 than to his own operas), Haydn also composed many insertion arias, either by way of a substitute for an existing number or simply to allow greater opportunities for his own company. Haydn's own operatic production was concentrated in the 1770s; only three works were to be composed for the Esterháza opera house in the following decade, the last of them, *Armida*, in 1783.

This falling-off was no coincidence. During these same years Haydn was becoming directly involved in the publication of his own works. On New Year's Day 1779 Haydn had signed a new contract with the Prince to replace that of 1761; its more relaxed and less prescriptive tone was an acknowledgment of the composer's greatly increased status both in his work-place and in the wider world. The most significant element was the suppression of the earlier document's fourth clause:

The said Vice-Capellmeister shall be under obligation to compose such music as His Serene Highness may command, and neither to communicate such compositions to any other person, nor to allow them to be copied, but he shall retain them for the absolute use of His Highness, and not compose for any other person without the knowledge and permission of His Highness.[1]

Its omission merely sanctioned the greater freedom of activity the composer was already enjoying; nevertheless, it meant Haydn was now more the master of his own destiny, at least in the instrumental sphere.

In addition to an increased publication rate, Haydn also received foreign commissions, resulting in such works as the 'Paris' Symphonies (Nos. 82–7), written in 1785–6 and commissioned by the Comte d'Ogny for the *Concert de la Loge Olympique*, and the concertos for the *lira organizzata* (a development of the hurdy-gurdy) for King Ferdinand IV of Naples. In 1780 he had begun his long association with Francesco and Carlo Artaria of Vienna, with the publication of the 'Op. 30' keyboard sonatas (five recently-written works, Nos. 48–52, plus the C minor Sonata of 1771). Business with the London firm of William Forster started a year later, through the mediation of General Charles Jermingham, British Ambassador at the Court of Vienna. (It should be borne in mind that publication then generally involved the issuing of parts rather than the appearance of a full score.)

Haydn was thus well aware of the demand for his music and was now taking a more direct role in the supply. He now also became more conscious of having a reputation to maintain, although, in spite of a good deal of adverse criticism, he remained an artist who did not so much respond to contemporary taste as create it – nowhere more so than in the string quartet. The later image of a perennially successful and universally loved composer is really only valid for the first decade of the nineteenth century, when Haydn was a retired celebrity rather than an active composer; prior to this, many assaults were mounted on his art, especially (but by no means exclusively) by the critics of north Germany. An instance of such hostilities may be observed in the comments of C. L. Junker, in a pamphlet entitled *Zwantzig Componisten, eine Skizze* of 1776, which was later reprinted in Leipzig in 1792:

Since the time when Hayde [*sic*] changed the tone of Viennese music, or set a new pace, it has actually become more characteristic than ever before, but from the dignity which it enjoyed under Wagenseil, it has too much sunk into triviality ... since Hayde, music has possibly suffered that very change that the theatre has also suffered, but the former certainly to less advantage.

... Had Hayden's [*sic*] caprice, by refining our taste, generally attempted to make music physically more beautiful, more attractive – had he really succeeded in this – then his original mixture would have brought him credit, – to the extent that it would have brought credit to music.

... No one will contradict that the only dominating attitude or (since we are dealing with music) the only dominating emotion in Hayden is eccentric, bizarre; – and projected without control. Will someone call to witness Hayden's Adagio? – good, then it's seriously committed caprice; like the tragic emotions of a Shakespear [!]. ... But just name me one single, solitary product of Hayden, in which caprice is not at the bottom of it all! You won't find any.[2]

However much the writer's attitudes may in themselves appear capricious and eccentric to us today, in an age when the sense of what is dangerous and exciting in Haydn's music has proved hard to recapture, we would do well to bear in mind such expressions of dismay. Interestingly, Junker found the quartets to be less scandalous in their expression than the symphonies.[3]

That Haydn was well aware of such criticisms may be seen in the defensive nature of some remarks in his letters; in 1780, writing to Artaria with regard to the Op. 30 Sonatas, he hoped that he would 'gain some honour by this work, at least with the judicious public; criticism of the works will be levelled only by those who are jealous (and there are many) ...' Two weeks later, he wrote again in connection with Op. 30:

Incidentally, I consider it necessary, in order to forestall the criticisms of any witlings, to print on the reverse side of the title page the following sentence, here underlined:

Avertissement
Among these 6 sonatas there are two single movements in which the same subject occurs through several bars: the author has done this intentionally, to show different methods of treatment.

For of course I could have chosen a hundred other ideas instead of this one; but so that the whole *opus* will not be exposed to blame on account of this one intentional detail (which the critics and especially my enemies might interpret wrongly), I think that this *avertissement* or something like it must be appended, otherwise the sale might be hindered thereby.[4]

Apart from showing a heightened awareness of 'market response', the letter is also notable for the almost military metaphor of 'my enemies'. This suggests that Haydn wanted to stay one step ahead of the opposition in his attempt to conquer the musical world (an attempt which we have seen was effected on both epistolary and musical levels in the case of Op. 33). This particular piece of correspondence may also reveal a certain creative insecurity about the twofold use of the theme in Op. 30: while the first movement of Sonata No. 52 in G major presents and develops the idea in a fairly successful manner, the companion A major middle movement of No.

49 is a flop in a work that would otherwise number amongst the composer's most successful keyboard works.

Just seventeen months later, in a letter to Artaria of 20 July 1781, Haydn is naming one of his 'enemies' more precisely, the composer Leopold Hofmann (in connection with the twelve lieder to be published in the same year);

You will find the words of the 4th, 8th and 9th *Lieder* in Friebert's *Lieder*, as published by Herr von Kurzböck, but in case you cannot get them, I shall send them to you. These 3 *Lieder* have been set to music by *Capellmeister* Hofmann, but between ourselves, miserably; and just because this braggart thinks that he alone has ascended the heights of Mount Parnassus, and tries to disgrace me every time with a certain high society, I have composed these very three *Lieder* just to show this would-be high society the difference . . .

. . . I pray you especially, good Sir, not to let anyone copy, sing, or in any way alter these *Lieder* before publication, because when they are ready, I shall sing them myself in the critical houses. By his presence and through the proper execution, the master must maintain his rights: these are only songs, but they are not the street songs of Hofmann, wherein neither ideas, expression nor, much less, melody appear.[5]

Haydn may thus be observed fighting a battle on several fronts during this decade; while he was attempting to exercise greater control over the dissemination and printed appearance of his works, he must have also struggled to keep up with the demands of the operatic season. The aggression of the Hofmann letter also suggests a certain hardening in the composer's attitude to the world. Toughness would certainly be required as Haydn's operatic duties became more onerous, reaching a peak about the time he started to compose Op. 50; there were 89 performances in 1785, 125 performances of seventeen operas (including 9 premieres) in 1786, and 98 performances of fourteen operas in 1787.[6] It is therefore rather appropriate that the Op. 50 set was to demonstrate a particular toughness of mind, indeed a touch of ruthlessness, in its execution.

4

Genesis

Composition

From 1781 thoughts of the string quartet can never have been far from Haydn's mind. The Op. 33 set in fact received a sort of 'command performance'[1] on Christmas Day of that year, in the apartments of Maria Feodorovna, wife of the Russian Grand Duke Paul. The royal couple was paying a visit to Vienna, and the attention thus given to Haydn can only have confirmed his newly-found sense of status in the musical and social world. The *Preßburger Zeitung* recorded the occasion thus (the Duke and Duchess travelled under the name 'von Norden'):

... We must add to our report of the concert given in Countess von Norden's rooms on December [25th] that the music was by the princely Esterhazy *Kapellmeister*, the famous Herr Hayden [*sic*], and that the quartet played on that occasion was performed by Messrs. Luigi Tomasini, Apfelmayr [Franz Aspelmayr], Weigl and [Thaddäus] Huber. It was received with gracious applause by the illustrious audience, who were pleased to present Herr Haydn, as composer, with a magnificent enamelled golden box set with brilliants, and each of the other four musicians with a golden snuff-box.[2]

A still more significant result of the appearance of these works was that they prompted another composer, Wolfgang Amadeus Mozart, to resume his efforts in the genre after a gap of nearly a decade (as was the case with Haydn). After being dismissed from the service of the Archbishop of Salzburg in 1781, Mozart had moved to Vienna, although when he first became acquainted with Haydn is unclear. The two composers may have met the day before the Op. 33 performance, when Mozart and Muzio Clementi engaged in a famous context of keyboard skills for the benefit of the royal visitors. Other opportunities for contact might have presented themselves in subsequent years, but it was probably not until 1784 that the composers had the chance to become firm friends. By 14 January 1785 Mozart had completed the last of the six quartets he was to dedicate to

Haydn, having written the first of them, K. 387 in G major, in 1782. The impact they made on the elder composer, who can previously have known very little, if any, of Mozart's music, may be measured by the famous remark made to Leopold Mozart describing Mozart *fils* as the greatest composer he knew; Haydn singled out 'taste' and 'knowledge of composition' as the touchstones of this judgment. The remark was made at a quartet party given by Mozart on 12 February 1785 to celebrate Haydn's initiation as a Freemason; in subsequent years Mozart and Haydn were to take every opportunity to play together in each other's string quartets (and in Mozart's quintets).

Haydn had of course exerted a musical influence on Mozart for many years; the six quartets of 1782–5 represented just another stage in this process, if evidently a more directly acknowledged one. The question of reciprocal influence has perhaps been overplayed, although many recent critics have drawn attention to just how slight Haydn's artistic reaction seems to have been. Jens Peter Larsen, for example, suggests of Op. 50 that 'if one did not know of Mozart's relations with Haydn one would scarcely see anything but Haydn in these quartets'.[3] Whatever the extent of the influence (the question will be raised again later on), contact with a composer of equal stature, for the first time in Haydn's life, must have sharpened his own sense of what he was about. This is apparent in the single D minor Quartet of 1785, which seems to represent the sole survivor from a set of three quartets 'intended for Spain', as Haydn wrote to Artaria on 5 April 1784.[4] (It was in fact published singly by Hoffmeister, a rival Viennese music publisher, and later acquired the designation 'Op. 42'.)

Whether or not Op. 42 was conditioned by the fact of writing for players whose standards Haydn could not estimate, it represents yet a further paring-down of musical resources. If indeed it can be viewed as any sort of response to the Mozartian quartet, then it only emphasizes the extent to which the composers were pursuing different ideals. The contrast is rather reminiscent of the exchange of views that took place when Mahler visited Sibelius in 1907, as related by the Finnish composer to his biographer:

When our conversation touched on the symphony, I said that I admired its style and severity of form, and the profound logic that created an inner connection between all the motifs. This was my experience in the course of my creative work. Mahler's opinion was just the opposite. 'No!' he said, 'The symphony must be like the world. It must be all-embracing.'[5]

Within limits, and with the notable and significant exception of the first of the six, K. 387, Mozart might have been affiliating himself with the Mahlerian position, putting all he knew into the set while Haydn pursued his own logic to an ever greater degree. In this respect, the 'Haydn' quartets may represent as much a re-engagement with Haydn's Op. 20, which Mozart imitated without enormous success in 1773, as a reaction to Op. 33; the lessons of the later set are perhaps better demonstrated in other works – in *The Marriage of Figaro*, for instance, completed in 1786. This shares with Op. 33 the feature that, whatever enticements we encounter along the way, the principal expressive agent is ultimately the sensation of inexorable forward movement, as if a new and more efficient mode of transport has suddenly been discovered.

The letter to Artaria in which Haydn mentioned the three 'Spanish quartets' also contains the first reference to the Op. 50 set:

Although I have always received more than 100 ducats for my quartets by subscription, and although Herr Willmann also promised to give me this sum, I agree to your offer of 300 fl. with the following stipulations; first that you are patient until July, though all six should be finished by then; secondly, I demand either 12 copies or my choice of the dedication.[6]

As we shall see, the 'choice of dedication' would take on a life of its own in 1787; in the meantime, Haydn appears to have been deflected from his intentions by other events, for in a letter to Artaria dated 18 May 1784 he writes simply: 'Regarding the quartets, the matter can wait'.[7] In the interim, of course, the 'Paris' Symphonies and *The Seven Last Words* demanded the composer's complete attention in his time off from operatic direction. Indeed, time had become so short for Haydn that in 1784 he perpetrated one of his more startling acts of dishonesty. While hard at work on his opera *Armida*, Haydn had received a request from Forster in London for three new piano trios. Anxious to accommodate the publisher and to secure the good price contingent upon a speedy delivery, Haydn mailed one of his own works, Trio No. 18 in G major, plus two that Pleyel had sent his former teacher from Strasbourg. Unfortunately for Haydn, the fraud was soon brought to Pleyel's attention, and when both composers found themselves in London in the next decade, a lawsuit against Haydn was eventually settled out of court.[8]

The first two quartets of Op. 50 were completed in February of 1787; the story of the dedication begins with a letter to Artaria of 27 February, in which Haydn refers to correspondence received from Konstantin Jacobi,

Prussian ambassador to Vienna. Jacobi had enquired about the progress of those compositions 'which Herr Artaria intends to send to the King at Berlin'.[9] Haydn continues: 'I hope that you do not intend to dedicate [*The Seven Last Words*] to His Majesty, either as quartets or for full band, because that would be contrary to all common sense; but I believe that you must mean the new Quartets, which I highly approve of, if this is what you intend to do.' On 7 March Haydn mentioned the matter again: 'Herr von Jacobi only wanted to know what work it was that you intended to dedicate to the King of Prussia, and I wrote to him that I believed it would be quartets.' The composer included with this letter the first movement of the Op. 50 third quartet.

A letter from the King himself, Friedrich Wilhelm II, written from Potsdam on 21 April, thanked Haydn for sending copies of the 'Paris' Symphonies:

His Majesty, King of Prussia, &c. &c. is sensible of the mark of respect which *Herr Kapellmeister* Haydn, in sending him six new Symphonies, again wishes to show to His Serene Majesty. They have especially pleased him, and there is no doubt that His Highness has always appreciated *Herr Kapellmeister* Haydn's works, and will appreciate them at all times. To provide concrete assurance of the same, he sends him the enclosed ring as a mark of His Highness' satisfaction and of the favour in which he holds him.

Naturally Haydn was honoured by this further sign of royal favour, and both the letter and the golden ring became treasured possessions, the ring sometimes doing service as a creative talisman. This gift now made the dedication of the quartets a straightforward matter, as Haydn wrote to Artaria on 19 May:

This is to inform you that I have already finished the 4th Quartet, and will certainly send it next Friday. Now here is something important I have to tell you: you know that I received a beautiful ring from His Majesty, the King of Prussia. I feel deeply in His Majesty's debt because of this present, and for my part I can think of no better and more fitting way to show my thankfulness to His Majesty (and also in the eyes of the whole world) than by dedicating these 6 quartets to him; but you won't be satisfied with that, because you will want to dedicate the works yourself, and to someone else. But to make amends for this loss, I promise to give you other pieces free of charge. Let me know what you have to say to this. Perhaps we can both be satisfied. In haste ...

Artaria evidently assented to this, for on 21 June Haydn wrote that the dedication ought to be formulated 'by some intelligent person in Vienna, but brief and to the point. The Minister, Herr von Jacoby, could assist you best of all.' The request for brevity and advice on assistance with the dedication (Haydn in fact confirmed the arrangement by writing to the ambassador himself) shows that Haydn had become not just a formidable businessman and marketer of his works, but an expert on form – of the social kind, this expertise in the musical domain having long been established. Prior to this, on 10 June 1787, Haydn had given a further progress report on the quartets – 'Since I shall complete the 5th Quartet this week, I assure you that you shall receive both Quartets in good order by a week from tomorrow, and finally the 6th in a short time' – but that these assurances were not be be realized reminds us of how many other activities were detaining the composer at the time. The 'in haste' which Haydn slipped in at the end of his letter of 19 May is confirmation of just how frenetic the tempo was at which he now had to conduct his affairs, and the correspondence of the following few months offers a vivid sense of this struggle. The letter of 21 June had also contained an assurance that the fourth and fifth quartets would reach Artaria 'on Sunday at the latest'; just two days later we read: 'I enclose the fourth Quartet, you will quite certainly receive the 5th this coming week.' Then, on 12 July, Haydn wrote 'I send you herewith the 6th Quartet. Lack of time prevented my having the 5th copied up to now, but I have composed it meanwhile.' The fifth quartet was not to be sent until 16 September – 'Because no safe opportunity presented itself, I could not send the enclosed Quartet before. Now, thank God! I am glad that I finished them at last' – and the sense of relief is palpable.

It is indicative of the premium Haydn had to put on his time that the proof-reading of the quartets took place not through perusal but by means of a performance, as the letter to Artaria of 7 October makes clear: 'At the first possible opportunity I shall send the Quartets, which I am having played this very day . . .'[10] In other words, Haydn had invited the principal string players from his orchestra to play through the works, so that any errors in engraving could be spotted aurally (Haydn's eyesight was to deteriorate within a few years). The two stages that preceded this are indicated by the letter of 12 July; Haydn first made a draft of his intentions, in a fairly full sketch-form, and later wrote down the entire score, furnished with the date and a signature. Most of the composer's extant autographs represent the latter stage; sketches, such as those for the G major slow movement of Op. 20 No. 3 and the Finale of Symphony No. 99, are much rarer.

Publication

Near the end of this period of composition and revision Haydn determined to profit doubly from his efforts. On 8 August he offered the six quartets and the six 'Paris' Symphonies to the London publisher William Forster for twenty-five guineas with the claim that neither set had yet been given to anyone, thus lying on both counts. Then, four days after sending Quartet No. 5 to Artaria, Haydn sent Forster copies of all six, for which he had evidently now signed a contract worth twenty guineas. As was the case with the two spurious piano trios, however, the deception was soon uncovered; the works were promptly published in London, leaving the more dilatory Viennese firm demanding an explanation from the opportunist of Esterháza.

At the same time Artaria was also losing out in its home market; the sale of unauthorized manuscript copies in Vienna enabled Haydn to avoid the issue in his next surviving letter to the firm. On 7 October Haydn confessed to being 'astonished at your penultimate letter concerning the theft of the Quartets. I assure you on my honour that they were not copied by my copyist, who is a most honest fellow, whereas your copyist is a rascal, for he offered mine 8 gold ducats this winter if he would give him the *Seven Words*.' The culprit in fact was the copyist Lorenz Lausch, who had perhaps bribed the selfsame 'rascal' in order to get hold of the works. Rather highhandedly in view of his own recent actions, Haydn suggested a means of discovering the criminal link: 'I am sorry not to be in Vienna myself so as to have him arrested: My plan would be to make Herr Lausch appear before Herr von Augusti, the mayor, and make him confess from whom he received the Quartets. Herr von Augusti is an old friend of mine and will certainly help you in this matter ...' The slightly forced tone of righteous indignation and the unexpected playing of two cards designed to place the composer on a moral high ground (the *Seven Words* incident together with a reminder of friends in high places) convey Haydn's anxiety to distance himself from any ideas of dishonest practice, not out of a sense of guilt but rather out of a determination to play his hand to the limit.

Soon, however, an informer in the guise of the London artist Gaetano Bartolozzi had confirmed the appearance of the Forster edition to Artaria, although Haydn simply denied the charge ('I don't know whether I should laugh or be angry ...'). But five days later, on 27 November, Haydn was forced to be more honest with his Viennese publishers, although he characteristically manipulated the situation so as to shift the blame away from himself:

You will forgive me, good Sir, that I have been unable to answer you sooner, for want of a good opportunity. You want me to give you a certificate ... for the 6 Quartets: I enclose it herewith. It is not true, however, that I gave a separate certificate to Herr Forster, giving him the sole rights to these works; but it is true that I sent one to him after the Quartets had already been engraved. It's your own fault, because you could have sent the quartets to Herr Langmann 3 months ago, and at the same time given him the sole rights. But your having held them back derives from your own great selfishness: no one can blame me for attempting to secure some profit for myself, after the pieces have been engraved: for I am not properly recompensed for my works, and have a greater right to get this profit than the other dealers. Therefore you will see that the contracts between us are more carefully drawn up, and that I am sufficiently remunerated. If you lose GENERALLY because of this, however, I shall find a way to compensate you in another way.

This letter initiated a period of estrangement between composer and publisher, although publication of Op. 50 went ahead the following month, being announced in the *Wiener Zeitung* of 19 December 1787. The title page read: SIX QUATUORS / POUR DEUX VIOLONS ALTO ET BASSE / Composés et dediés / A Sa Majesté / FREDERIC GUILLAUME II / ROI DE PRUSSE / par / IOSEPH HAYDN / Œuvre 50me / a Vienne chez Artaria Compagnie ...' Not long after, the firm sent Haydn some 'excellent cheese' and sausages, and, although the composer gratefully acknowledged these presents in a letter of 16 February 1788, the rift remained. This much is apparent in a letter sent to William Forster on 28 February after Haydn had learnt of his troubles with 'Langmann', the London firm of Longman & Broderip and Artaria's business partners, who in the normal course of events would have expected to publish the string quartets themselves. Haydn begins: 'Don't be angry at me that you have disagree-ableness with Herr Langmann. I shall make it up to you another time. It's not my fault but the usurious practices of Herr Artaria. This much I can promise you: that as long as I live neither Artaria or Langmann shall have anything from me, directly or indirectly.' Once more the composer steps adroitly out of the firing-line, as he portrays himself as the victim of others' greed rather than the exploiter of it that he had undoubtedly become. He continues with a statement that we can only read with a heavy sense of irony: 'I am too honest and straightforward to want to hurt your feelings or to damage you.' There is irony not only in view of the immediate context surrounding this protestation of honour but also in the longer term: not only did Haydn 'get away with it', comparatively speaking, during his lifetime, but his posthumous reputation has always remained largely untainted by these duplicities. Honesty and straightforwardness have become part of the lore surrounding Haydn both as a man and as a composer.

As if this protestation were not outrageous enough in the circumstances, Haydn, quite unbowed by his situation and only a few sentences into the letter, is suddenly looking to secure a moral and financial advantage: 'But you certainly must realize that whoever wants to have the exclusive rights for 6 new pieces of mine must pay more than 20 guineas. In fact I have recently signed a contract with someone who pays me 100 and more guineas for each 6 works.'[11] What should have been an exercize in damage limitation is quickly turned by Haydn into an opportunity to gain more favourable rates for future works. Altogether this letter, like so many others by Haydn, demonstrates the same turn of mind that informs the Op. 50 quartets themselves: one that is able to formulate ideas with great brevity, then move quickly and relentlessly onward in order to achieve its own ends.

Whether one is amused by the effrontery or scandalized by the impropriety of Haydn's commercial behaviour, the extenuating circumstances must be understood. Haydn's drive to capitalize on his musical products was fuelled, as we have seen, by the realization that he had been denied any part in the profits made for many years under his name. Once he did begin to gain some reward for his efforts, it was only too natural that he would want to 'catch up' on his lost earnings, to acquire by any means that which years of endeavour had failed to yield. That Haydn suffered under a sense of rough justice is apparent in his confrontational letter to Artaria of 27 November 1787 ('I ... have a greater right to get this profit than the other dealers'); all his own dealings of the time combine such affirmations of principle with a distinctly unprincipled opportunism (although Haydn, in his way, no doubt saw one as the logical consequence of the other, given the business environment in which he had to operate). Indeed, it was Haydn's aggressive insistence on his rights and growing appreciation of his 'clout' that was initiating a major change in the status of composers. The major credit in this process is commonly given to Beethoven, just as many of Haydn's musical innovations are still associated with their imitation in his pupil's works;[12] the new ground he broke seemingly unnoticed was to be reclaimed by Beethoven, but without the same guile or amiable public persona with which to cover his tracks.

Haydn had, however, a much more specific reason for being less than forthright with Artaria when it came to the publication of string quartets. The grand appearance of his previous set, Op. 33, had nearly been sabotaged by the announcement of their publication on 29 December 1781, thus embarrassing Haydn with his obligations to the 'exclusive' subscribers to the set. Haydn's subsequent letter of 4 January 1782 has a familiar ring to it:

To my astonishment I read in the Vienna Diario that you intend to publish my Quartets in 4 weeks; I wish you had shown sufficient consideration for me to delay the announcement until I had left Vienna: such a proceeding places me in a most dishonourable position and is very damaging; it is a most usurious step on your part. At least you could have waited with the announcement until the whole *opus* was completed, for I have not yet satisfied all my subscribers: Mons. Hummel also wanted to be a subscriber, but I did not want to behave so shabbily, and I did not want to send them to Berlin wholly out of regard for our friendship and further transactions; and by God! you have damaged me to the extent of more than 50 ducats, since I have not yet satisfied many of the subscribers, and cannot possibly send copies to many of those living abroad. This step must cause the cessation of all further transactions between us.[13]

Haydn took just sixteen days to reconsider the matter; he did not soften his stance with regard to Op. 50 for six months. On 22 May 1788 he wrote 'I shall never forget that you gave me preference over many', adding significantly 'though I well know that I occasionally deserved it more than the others'.[14] In any case, by his counter-dealings with Forster Haydn had increased his prospects of financial success and, perhaps, secured a measure of unconscious revenge.

5

The story of the autographs

The involved circumstances that seem to have attended the Op. 50 string quartets at each stage of their history are remarkable enough in themselves, and few parallels can be found elsewhere in Haydn's output. It is all the more appropriate, therefore, that an extraordinary new chapter should have been added to this story within the past ten years. In the absence of any surviving contemporary or near-contemporary criticism of the works and in the context of the comparative neglect of the set, the reappearance in 1982 of the autographs of Nos. 3 to 6 has allowed the opus to reassert itself with a vengeance; the four works concerned can boast a tale whose richness and improbability are second to none. Not only do these autographs show many substantial differences from the standard editions, but, just as importantly, their recent reappearance provides for us a vivid and direct link with the past. At the same time, from both a musical and a documentary point of view, the works have also now acquired a new freshness and relevance to the present.[1]

The beginning of this story suggests that the celebration of composers' anniversaries may after all have its positive side. Thus the fact that in 1982 Haydn turned two hundred and fifty years old, as it were, prompted the organization of a Haydn Festival in Melbourne to which the conductor Christopher Hogwood was invited. At the end of a concert given on a wet Sunday afternoon in Melbourne's Universal Theatre, featuring works of various genres from Haydn's London years, Hogwood was approached by a 'little old lady' bearing what she thought might be some authentic Haydn manuscripts in a plastic shopping bag. After telling Hogwood briefly about the history of the documents and allowing some pages to be photocopied in the manager's office of the theatre, she disappeared.

At the risk of removing some of the colour from this early part of the story – although there will be sufficient later by way of compensation – it must be said that there was an element of 'good copy' about the reports of this incident. An account in a local newspaper, *The Age*, was read out on the

ABC radio programme 'Arts Illustrated' with a request for the diminutive and venerable woman to make contact with the Australian Broadcasting Commission. It was her husband who made the call, pointing out with some vehemence that the 'little old lady' was 'no old lady' but his wife, a robust and definitely middle-aged fifty-three-year-old. In addition, the plastic bag was employed not out of any casual disregard for the potential musical importance of the pages contained therein but for the purpose of anonymity; furthermore, inside the shopping bag the autographs were placed in a jiffy bag, so that they were doubly protected. Indeed, the false implications of the initial media image, irresistible though it must have been, provide a nice parallel with the fate of the four works themselves before these very autographs came to light: that of a text distorted according to what subsequent editors thought ought to have happened rather than what did.

A further fortunate consequence of the anniversary of the composer's birth was the organization of a Haydn conference in Adelaide in May of 1982. Dr Georg Feder, director of the Haydn Institute in Cologne, was interviewed the day after his arrival for the conference by Mr Tony Cane of the ABC. When told of the incident in Melbourne, Feder was properly cautious, but his scepticism vanished when, a few weeks later, he finally made contact with the owners. The day before his departure from the country was spent at the house of the owners, making a more detailed examination of the autographs, first of all from a text-critical point of view; they were then laid on a clear glass plate illuminated by a lamp below in order to check watermarks and the rastrography (the ruling of the staves). The works were written on Italian manuscript paper, in oblong format with ten systems per page, such as was commonly to be had in the Vienna of the time.

The following day, Feder continued his textual comparisons with the standard editions of the quartets, but, running out of time before a mid-afternoon flight back to Germany, requested that he be allowed to take photocopies with him. This was achieved, to return to the 'little old lady' level of the story, by dashing to the local public library on a Saturday morning to copy the rest of the one hundred and twenty-six pages (No. 6 had been duplicated the previous day). A long and perhaps long-suffering queue formed behind, unaware of the crucial efforts taking place in front and no doubt frustrated when at midday a bell announced the end of the day's business. However, the mission had been accomplished, and a few hours later Feder gave a press conference at Melbourne airport (covered by ABC television) confirming the discovery of the autographs to the world.

The hectic tempo of these events contrasts markedly with the more leisurely life that the autographs had led up to that point. They remained in the composer's possession after publication and appear in Johann Elssler's catalogue of Haydn's music library compiled in 1804–5. On Haydn's death in 1809 they were purchased, at least nominally, by Prince Nicolaus Esterházy II, the fourth and last of Haydn's noble patrons; this fulfilled the terms of a private agreement, made between the two men in 1807, that the Prince would buy all the composer's musical effects. From this point we have no solid information about their fate until 1851. In that year they were sold at a London auction house to an English colonel, who, about to emigrate with his family to New Zealand, evidently bought the manuscripts as a form of security in the event of hard times ahead. In 1852 the family travelled on the second voyage of the 'Jane Seymour', the colonel taking with him the autographs and his Amati violin; they settled in Christchurch, then as now the most Anglophile of New Zealand cities, where the colonel appears to have set up his own orchestra. As he also had four musical daughters, it seems likely that the first 'authentic' performances of the four works must have taken place privately in the middle of the nineteenth century, precisely half-way round the world from the place of their conception!

At the same time our proud owner must have decided that he wanted to preserve the separate manuscript pages in a more permanent form, and he had them bound into one volume with a handsome red cover. On the front, in gold lettering, stands 'Autograph Quartettes/Haydn', with the name of the owner in the left-hand corner; on the inside of the front cover is affixed the name of the printers, 'G. Tombs & Co./Printers/&/Bookbinders,/ Christchurch'. Into the volume the colonel had his own especially devised contents page inserted; this contains *incipits* for each of the four quartets, with page references to the right. On the left-hand side are written in pencil the equivalent numbers in the 'Litoff' [*recte*: Litolff] edition, 46–9, which the colonel clearly possessed either in score or in parts. Most intriguingly, near the foot of the page is the note 'The interlineations "VV", "Viola" "Violoncello" &c are Clementi's writing', which provides the only clue as to the fate of the autographs from the time of their purchase in 1809 to their appearance at auction in 1851. These annotations, which are in fact in Clementi's hand, were necessitated by the fact that the autograph pages had been trimmed, including the removal of the two empty staves at the bottom of each page. It is of course possible that it was Clementi himself who cut off the paper for his own use. Since Clementi died in 1832, the whereabouts of the autographs in the following two decades remains a mystery.

A more crucial question, however, is how the manuscript reached London in the first place. The most likely agent of its removal is Johann Nepomuk Hummel, the composer who was in effect Haydn's successor: in 1804 he was engaged by Prince Nicolaus II as *Concertmeister* (the other part of Haydn's job was covered by the appointment of a Johann Nepomuk Fuchs as Vice-*Capellmeister* to direct the church music). Since the Prince disliked Esterháza, spending the summers in Eisenstadt and the winters in Vienna, he asked Hummel to sort through all the music there, including of course the works that would form part of Haydn's estate, and bring the useful material to Eisenstadt.

Thus Hummel acquired his own 'unofficial' collection of Haydn autographs, and at some point he may have laid hands on Op. 50. He was dismissed by the Prince in 1811, but if he took the works to London himself it could not have been until 1830, when he visited the city for the first time in nearly forty years. We do know that Hummel took many other Haydn manuscripts to England; most have since found a home in the British Museum (now British Library). If the autographs of Op. 50 were taken on this particular journey, then they must have passed directly to Clementi, who retired in that year and was, of course, to die two years later.

Another possibility is that Clementi acquired the autographs himself on one of his many trips to the Continent. After his *Wanderjahre* in Europe, Clementi was based in Vienna from the end of 1808 until 1810, when he returned to London. He would certainly have visited the frail Haydn some time before the latter's death on 31 May 1809, not just to pay his respects but also as a business acquaintance (he had been publishing a number of Haydn's works). There exists the faint possibility that Haydn made a gift of the autographs to Clementi – he is known to have given some of his manuscript works away in later years – but a more likely sequence of events would involve Clementi receiving the works from Hummel, perhaps as part of a business transaction. There would also have been later opportunities – four more visits to the Continent before his retirement – for Clementi to have acquired the works in such a manner. Aside from these speculations, there remain other questions, such as the ownership of the autographs subsequent to Clementi, the reason for their being auctioned, and the manner of and reason for the separation of Nos. 1 and 2 from their companions (they remain lost to the present day).

Once the autographs arrived on the other side of the world, however, their history is much clearer. On the colonel's death they passed to his grand-daughter and, indeed, to a location even more remote from the Old World of their inception. The bound volume was kept in a bookcase on a sheep station in the South Island. There, in a majestic setting, remote in another sense from the flat landscape around Esterháza, they peacefully bided their time. The grand-daughter even had the works placed on microfilm and stored in the Alexander Turnbull Library in Wellington; rather surprisingly, this responsible custodial act did not provide the autographs with their breakthrough into the public domain. Shortly before her death in 1975 the works passed to her half-sister, the present owner. As the latter had by then shifted to Melbourne, however, the autographs had to be fetched, and the manner in which this was accomplished introduces another note of incongruity that Haydn would have relished. A daughter of the owner happened to be on holiday in New Zealand at the time, and, having picked up the autographs, she packed them in a suitcase and simply continued her trip. Thus the autographs went on tour, as it were, around the country in which they had spent most of their lives, before reaching their new home several weeks later. Once there, they were literally stored under a bed in a jiffy bag. The scores would be brought out on occasion to show to friends, or the family would follow them while listening to the recordings made by the Tokyo String Quartet. (This is another respect in which Op. 50 has recently been blessed, for these performances, recorded around the time the autographs moved from New Zealand, represent Haydn playing of unsurpassed excellence – in spite of the drawback of their reliance on a 'standard' edition.) The autographs were even shown to an established string quartet in Australia, but again to no great effect.

Thus it is clear that neither the owners, past and present, nor those who had been given access to the autographs had quite realized the precise documentary value of what they were looking at. Through their own efforts the present owners had become aware of the existence of a number of other copies without understanding the pre-eminence of theirs, Haydn's own fair copy representing obviously the most important evidence for his compositional intentions. What they were not to know was that none of the other copies was in Haydn's hand and that all consisted of separate parts rather than the full score. These authentic copies consist of: a set now housed in the Esterházy Archive of the National Library in Budapest; the parts sent to Forster on 20 September 1787; the first Artaria and Forster editions; and, most significantly, the manuscript parts from Haydn's library which passed through the hands of one J. N. Hummel before being bought from his legacy by the British Museum.[2] Hummel's possession of these copies (except for the parts to No. 3, another mysterious 'blip' in the history of the opus) strengthens the likelihood that he played some part in the fate of the autograph scores.

Now that the autographs have at last reappeared, however, some indication may be given of the revelations they contain. These naturally vary in scope. As compared with the standard editions, over one thousand dynamic, articulation and phrasing marks should be added or – more commonly – deleted. But other details are of much wider significance. Perhaps the most remarkable of these are the *Sieg[ue]* indications that appear at the end of the middle movements of No. 6; Haydn is thus directing that the final three movements be played without a break. This could be taken to indicate a particularly close relationship between the Poco adagio, Menuetto, and finale, although it could hardly be maintained that No. 6 is any more tightly unified than the other works. There is a more compelling large-scale reason why Haydn should have chosen to make the movements abut on each other: the ensuing emphasis on continuity and forward drive is peculiarly appropriate to the character of this particular work as a whole. However, this issue can only be dealt with properly in later chapters.

Another matter of structural import is raised by the autograph version of the third movement of No. 5 (see Illustration 3). This differs radically from the form found in the standard editions, as explained by Georg Feder:

In the traditional text it is headed Menuetto and Trio. Following the F major Minuet, the Trio is in F minor and has the usual two sections, both furnished with repeat-marks. In the original manuscript the movement is entitled 'Tempo di Menuet', and the middle section carries no title. A further difference is that the first section of this so-called Trio is not marked to be repeated; in addition, the Trio has no F-minor key-signature but continues in F major, only turning to the new tonality in the third bar with a *forzando*.

How was the traditional version arrived at? Through a process of misunderstanding and false analogy. This was initiated by the first Paris edition, published by Sieber in 1788. While printing the original text in all its essentials, Sieber placed the dot after the quaver rest in the first violin so close to the double bar found at the end of the first 'Trio' section that Richomme, the engraver of parts for the Pleyel edition, took

1 The slow movement of No. 3, bars 1–18: Haydn's autograph (in private possession, Melbourne)

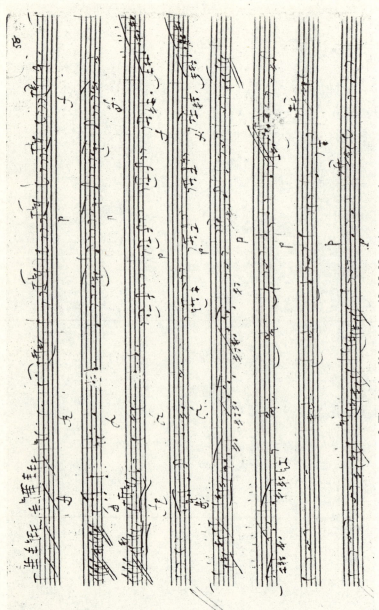

2 The finale of No. 4, bars 69–85: Haydn's autograph

3 The minuet and trio of No. 5, bars 38–57: Haydn's autograph

it to indicate repeat marks. Thus in the first violin part at the end of the section, Pleyel printed repeat marks before the double bar instead of the dot following the quaver rest. Moreover, he changed the D in the first whole bar to Db in all the parts to bring it into line with the following Db. Yet it was precisely the F major tonality at the beginning of the 'Trio' that caused Haydn to dispense with the change of key-signature, and the omission of a repeat for the first part had everything to do with this D, which, were it to be played again after the Ab major close of the first part, would put the music at cross-purposes with itself.

Subsequent editions went further down the same logical path, so to speak. Imbault (about 1807–10) restored, as did Pleyel's *Edition nouvelle*, the missing dot in the first-violin part and, like Pleyel's edition in score, put repeat marks in all parts and then added them at the beginning of the section. The editor of the Leipzig edition of Hoffmeister & Kühnel (around 1804) did the same. Moreover he did not see why a piece that was apparently in F minor should not be prefaced with a key signature, and he proceeded to add one. In addition he inserted the 'Trio' heading.[3]

Haydn's original intentions, before being buried under the editorial accretions described by Feder, are once more of significance for the whole work: the horizontal dissonance, as it were, of D and Db forms a central climax to the use of C♯/Db as an intrusive device through all three tonic-key movements. (The Doblinger edition has not taken account of this revelation.)

One more example may be given at this point of the manner in which one small error of musical reproduction can lead to further layers of distortion, if on a more modest scale. This concerns the finale of No. 6, where in bar 134 of the autograph Haydn writes an e[1] for the second violin, so that the G major subdominant harmony of the previous bar is transformed into an E minor 6–3 chord. Georg Feder once more takes up the story:

The version in the original manuscript was followed by the authorized copies [now] in Budapest and London, the first editions in London and Vienna and the reprint by Hummel. The Paris reprint of Sieber differs: he prints d[1], as in the previous bar, instead of e[1]. The G major chord that results from this misprint, the same chord as that of the previous bar, is unobtrusive, if not exactly ideal according to the rules of harmony, since it leads to hidden parallel fifths with the cello over into the following bar. Aesthetically speaking, the reiteration of the G major chord results in a disappointing drop in voltage, although it seems to correspond to bars 127–128; and so the mistake persisted. Pleyel followed Sieber, but rightly found the repetition of the d[1] pointless when set against the viola and cello parts; therefore he tied the two notes together. This is a typical case of plausible but false conjecture; it did not occur to Pleyel that the second d[1] might be revised to an e[1], and he did not consult other sources. Imbault and the Leipzig Bureau de Musique of Kühnel, predecessor of the Peters edition, followed Pleyel. The editors of Peters made a further conjecture: in order somehow to provide the G major chord, held for two bars, with the requisite intensity, they added a *fz* to its entry in bar 133 (and did the same to bar 127). This is of course merely an extrinsic substitute, bearing no comparison to the inner force that arises naturally from the change of harmony in bar 134. Eulenburg follows the false Peters version.[4]

Such are the false trails which led further and further away from Haydn's real intentions.

6

Critical reception

In most discussions of the set, Op. 50 has been treated as another link in the grand chain left by the 'father of the string quartet'; thus, finding itself in the middle of the *oeuvre*, it has received a disproportionate amount of inattention. In their comprehensive surveys many authors, having dwelt for so long on Opp. 20 and 33, accelerate past the succeeding sets to arrive in good time at Opp. 76 and 77, Haydn's last eight completed quartets. (Only the two middle movements of Op. 103 were completed for publication.) The progress theory has played its part in this tendency; coming at the end of the line, Opp. 76 and 77 have been fortunate in being treated mostly on their own merits, relatively unconditioned by a context of past and future achievements. There is, naturally, an inevitable danger that any wide stylistic account of musical works of art will lead, in the words of Carl Dahlhaus, to their being 'perceived less in aesthetic terms, as self-contained creations, than as documentary evidence on an historical process taking place by means of and through them'.[1] This process of the individual work submitting to a collective force is all the more noticeable when, as in the case with Op. 50, the existing literature rarely treats the music in great detail.

The set has proved particularly susceptible to the adoption of a 'bird's-eye view', given the striking economy of its musical procedures; 'monothematicism' has thus figured prominently in accounts of Op. 50. Commentators such as Reginald Barrett-Ayres, Jens Peter Larsen, and Rosemary Hughes have concentrated on this feature, although differing in their interpretations of the result: does the musical argument encourage us to hear purposefulness or versatility in the economy? For Larsen the set strikes a 'fine balance between unity and infinite variety'.[2] Hughes cleverly relates its procedures to the composition of the *Seven Last Words* in 1786; this produced music that was 'monothematic both spiritually and musically',[3] to be reflected immediately in the quartets of the following year. Another revealing comparison is drawn by Paul Griffiths: while the

'Paris' symphonies of 1785–6 are 'full of characterful ideas', Op. 50 'mark[s] an extreme in the submergence of themes so that arguments can be the richer and more prominent'.[4] Thus for Griffiths the 'unity' does not consist so much in the constant reiteration of one idea (although one wonders how even a single theme can be 'submerged' if its presence is so vital to the discourse) as in the linearity of procedure that the reiterations establish.

Karl Geiringer takes the monothematic process to be a manifestation of a character trait and a natural culmination of Haydn's own musical instincts: those movements that 'seem hewn from a single block' represent the most 'complete expression of [Haydn's] straightforward and undivided personality'. Such a judgment of character on the basis of the composer's technique and formal predilections has been frequently echoed in the literature; pleasingly, though, it has been less in evidence in recent times, giving way to a renewed appreciation of the radical nature of Haydn's achievement. In the present case, for instance, Haydn's procedures are surely far too obsessive, and at the same time too quick-witted, to qualify as an expression of solidity or straightforwardness. It must be understood that Haydn was both extreme and isolated in this respect; that he was able to dominate and indeed constitute the mainstream in spite of his rigorous musical philosophy is a paradox central to the understanding of his achievement.

Geiringer proceeds from the above character assessment to describe Op. 50 as a 'rather serious and thoughtful series';[5] Paul Griffiths assents, noting that with the disappearance of much of the comedy of Op. 33 the set is 'once more a collection of "serious" quartets', but without 'declaim[ing] its profundity in the manner of op. 20'.[6] Charles Rosen notes that the set is 'grander' than its predecessor and 'as a whole represents a solidification and an expansion of the light-hearted revolutionary procedures of op. 33'. While rightly emphasizing the greater breadth of musical argument in the 1787 works, these commentaries rather slight the sense of fun that runs through the opus. Of course there are exceptions – the F♯ minor Quartet, confined in its restless private world, hardly smiles at all, and the slow movements, as Rosen notes, are more predisposed to a 'tranquil gravity' than before.[7] Yet the most significant shift from Op. 33 is simply the level at which the humour is experienced – or, rather, the wit that now predominates over the 'comedy'. Practical jokes are still played, most obviously in the trios of Nos. 1 and 2, but the sense of fun is now more likely to be a product of the musical procedures rather than the starting-point it often was in 'Gli Scherzi', as Op. 33 became known.

A subtle example can be found in the opening theme of Op. 50 No. 3, whose wit in construction far surpasses the relaxed good humour of the material itself. Having said all that is needed for a complete harmonic unit by the second bar, with all-too-solid I–V and V–I cadences, the rest of the theme consists of deliberately feeble attempts to fill out a conventional eight-bar frame. First of all that time-honoured means of musical extension, a sequence, is initiated but leads to an impasse on a repeated first-inversion tonic chord (bar 4). The violins now break the rules by introducing in effect a brand new theme, a rustic strain that bears no relationship to the incisive opening gambit; the textural and timbral incongruity (octaves are far too 'unbuttoned' for this point in the form) also plays its part. The two lower instruments are only too ready to agree to this new space-filling proposition (bars 6^6–8^4), and thus the eighth-bar goal is reached. Having rather scrambled to this point, having lost face in spite of all good intentions at the start, the four players assess the damage. A family row breaks out, as it were, with the two musical elements now heard simultaneously; the viola is particularly truculent, while the cello clings to an E♭ throughout the passage (bars 9–12) in an attempt to provide a note of stability.

Such creative playfulness and wit of procedure are found throughout the set. A number of commentators, however, have seen the quartets rather as a strategic combination of the outstanding features of the two preceding sets. Orin Moe, Jr, for instance, regards Op. 50 as 'the first set to contain all the essential elements of [Haydn's] mature style'[8] and defines the mixture thus:

To a large extent, Op. 33 reduces the intense concern of Op. 20 with equal-voice texture, elaborate counterpoint, and soloistic display. Opus 50 revives this concern and unites it with the accomplishments of Op. 33 ... The lightness of Op. 33 does not disappear entirely, but it yields much to learning and complexity.[9]

Such a summary, while useful from a broad stylistic viewpoint, finally distorts the significance of Op. 50 by assigning it a conservative role; the sense that its mission was to combine lightness of touch with substance of material produces an identikit music that is 'solidly humorous'. Such a concept is not only foreign to the spirit of Haydn altogether but also overlooks the demonic zeal with which the composer pursues his musical ends in this particular set; rather than being more 'balanced' than the two previous groups, it is arguably less so. Not only do 20 and 33 not add up to 50, but the proposed musical equation is also unsound.

The critical emphasis on monothematicism is also misleading unless it is further qualified. For one thing, it is not the procedure that involves the restatement of an opening idea in the dominant more or less verbatim, such that the reiteration acts as an agent of formal stability (see for instance the outer movements of Symphony No. 104). The application of the term in this context cannot speak for the variety of material that may be found elsewhere in the exposition or whole movement. In addition it must be understood that in Op. 50 Haydn does not really proceed from a single idea, in the sense of representing one unified impulse. Rather, and more consistently than anywhere else in his output, he starts with one multi-idea: as László Somfai defines it, the selection of 'conflicting material as the starting point for movements that are driven on solely through the liberation and unfolding of the musical energies hidden within them'.[10]

In this sense, a kind of dual thematic impulse may be said to be already inherent in the opening themes; indeed, this was overt in the theme of No. 3 described above. All six opening themes in fact find ways of defeating our expectations: they contain problematic or contradictory elements which demand Haydn's exclusive attention if resolution is to be achieved. Indeed, the insistence on the thorough working-out of an initial problem has implications beyond the confines of the opening movements – the sense of unity in each whole work, as Rosen notes with respect to No. 4, has 'grown immensely'.[11] Not only are the opening 'problems' readdressed in subsequent movements, but the profile of the theme itself now determines many aspects of the whole work: harmonic rhythm, phrase-structure, texture, and its characteristic sonority. Rosen affirms this crucial aspect of the group with reference to the first movements of Nos. 1 and 6. After extensive analyses of both movements in *The Classical Style*, he writes:

The difference between the expositions of these two quartets does not imply freedom or variety in the usual sense, but comes from a new conception of the demands of the material, the central idea. A long and completely separate tonic section in the B flat Quartet above arises from the opening tonic pedal, while the uninterrupted flow of the D major Quartet's exposition is in answer to the tension at the beginning which immediately directs the music towards the dominant of the dominant. It should be noted that, because of this impulsion, there is no cadence on the dominant until almost the end of the exposition: again, this is not a whimsical evasion of normal practice, but a sensitivity to musical forces ... In both these works, as in almost all of Haydn from 1780 on, the most eccentric musical ideas (and both works are astonishing) are purged of mannerism by an understanding and a display of their full musical significance.[12]

Likewise, Somfai refers to the fact that 'unlike other Haydn opuses containing six works, there is absolutely no opening movement of a type to give a decisive character to the series'. As well as the two Allegro movements in Nos. 1 and 6, whose fundamental differences Rosen has elucidated above, there are also the 'rhythmic extremes' of the 'easy-flowing' Nos. 3 and 5, in 6/8 and 2/4 respectively, while '[t]he most fascinating contrast ... is evident in the movements in 3/4 time: in contrast to the asymmetric sentences and playful surprises reminiscent of opera buffa, that occur in the Vivace 3/4 (C major), the Spiritoso 3/4 (F sharp minor) is propelled by a stubborn ostinato rhythm'.[13]

We thus arrive at another paradoxical feature of the set: that while Haydn is unprecedentedly strict and determinist in his approach to the individual work, on the level of the whole opus he appears to enjoy more freedom of action than ever. Donald Tovey, in one of the earliest comprehensive surveys of the quartets, seemed to recognize as much when, upon arriving at the first work of Op. 50, he pronounced:

Pitiful will be the subterfuges of the teacher or student who succeeds in making out that the first movement of our next quartet ... has a 'second subject' and a recapitulation; nor will orthodoxy be saved by saying 'this is form in the making, before these things were differentiated'. It is form in the highest state of efficiency, freedom, and terseness, long after every element has been differentiated. From Op. 50 onwards there is no dealing with Haydn's first movements except by individual analysis.[14]

Haydn thus seems to have manoeuvred himself into a position from which he could enjoy greater liberty through the exercise of greater logic. This combination makes life hard for the critic who would differentiate between the accomplishments of each successive set of quartets, since while Haydn appears on the surface to give with one hand while taking away with the other, in reality he has defeated us through his *legerdemain*. David Wyn Jones, in connection with Op. 50, defines this elusive versatility thus: 'it was Haydn's unparalleled achievement, and it is our problem of comprehension, that each set is significant, and almost every work a rigorous investigation of the possibilities of the medium'.[15]

7

Design

The mixture of rigour and freedom with which Haydn approached the task of writing six new string quartets in 1787 can easily be obscured by any overview of the set. By their very nature, summary descriptions are liable to emphasize the consistencies rather than the variations in a composer's approach; in terms of its critical reception, Op. 50 has thus tended to be marginalized under the heading of 'monothematicism'. This, as has been pointed out, is a natural enough tendency; the variety, on the other hand, can only be appreciated by investigating each work and movement on its own terms. In the case of the first movements this imbalance is easily remedied. The fact that they all employ what has come to be known as sonata form is of far less interest than the diversity of material and technique that they employ, as Somfai and Rosen have affirmed; and the following approaches to Op. 50 will be less concerned with this formal aspect of the first movements than with the model they provide for the musical action of the entire work. Indeed, sonata form itself in the Classical period must be understood not as a set of specific structural demands, as in the old textbook definitions, but as a principle that may apply to any external design. This sonata principle involves a sensitivity to the balance of stable and unstable elements – not just harmonic, but also motivic and textural – in which the instability is concentrated towards the middle of the formal arch and the stability is established particularly towards the end of the structure.

This sense of proportion and dramatic shaping may seem so natural as to be applicable to all sorts and styles of music, but the fact is that only the Classical style pursues this goal as the ultimate agent of musical structure. Thus, tensions have to be *heard* to lessen, the seemingly irrational has to be rationalized, and forms must appear rounded and closed. Elements of ambiguity may not normally be left unresolved – certainly not at the level of the whole work, although individual movements may indeed leave something more to be said. Should the composer deliberately choose to withhold the final degree of resolution from individual movements, then the finale, which by its nature cannot leave matters unsettled, assumes a more specific importance in the multi-movement scheme.

Given Haydn's predilection for disturbing Classical proprieties in Op. 50, not just in the opening but also in subsequent movements, it is not surprising that the role of the finale now finds a new clarity. The 'mono-thematic' mould in which the finales are cast is thus a consequence of this role rather than simply a product of the earlier thematic rigour. While rehearsing the patterns and problems of previous movements, the finale must find ways of regularizing and again resolving them. Consequently the rondo structures which sustained all of the finales of the Op. 33 set except one[1] are set aside in favour of more densely argued sonata forms; while the Op. 33 finales had an element of the character piece about them, their Op. 50 equivalents present a more direct response to preceding events. The increased feeling for unity in the set has already been remarked upon: the strengthened sense of the part individual movements may play in the presentation of a larger thesis is nowhere more evident than in these final movements.

The finales are thus not only literally but also more metaphorically an expression of the sonata principle, which is now applied not just in an individual but also in a more collective sense. Their example only confirms that the most remarkable and individual aspect of the Classical style is not the way in which material is developed but rather the way in which it is *resolved*. 'Motivic development' is often thought to be the most decisive achievement of the style, but many of the techniques employed to this end (such as the use of sequence) had already been absorbed by the Baroque idiom. Equally, while the nineteenth-century Romantic era continued and extended the practice, so that it in turn became arguably the ultimate agent of musical structure, the era had greater difficulty in defining an alternative aesthetic for the problem of formal closure – simply, of how to finish a large-scale work. The preceding style had accepted fully the ideal of a closed, self-sufficient system in which all elements of disorder are resolved with a thoroughness and indeed consistency that earned it its 'Classical' label.

While the Op. 50 finales address the issues of Classical proportion and resolution in an unprecedentedly direct way, Haydn nevertheless manages to give them a secure identity of their own so that they do not function solely as completions of a larger thought-process. Ironically enough, Haydn achieves this in four cases by proceeding from a theme that sounds as if it will introduce a rondo form. This is a matter of proportions: rondo-type themes normally have a regular rhythmic manner and squareness of phrasing which, together with a straightforward diatonic diction, prepare us for a regularity and ease of return through the course of the movement. This taste for making us 'expect a form, not in view of his successive structural events, but in view of the sheer character of his themes', as Hans Keller explains the device,[2] is found in other Haydn genres of the time, such as the finales of Symphony No. 83 of 1785 or Piano Trio No. 27 from about 1789. Just to increase the confusion in the latter instance, Haydn actually marks the movement 'Rondo'!

The two Op. 50 finales without rondo implications in their thematic make-up find other ways of asserting their independence: No. 4 presents a fugue which provides a distinct climax to, as much as a resolution of, the previous movements, while No. 6 proceeds from the technique of *bariolage* to constitute the most singular movement of the whole set. In any case, however the composer chooses to characterize each finale, its resolving nature involves more than the reiteration of earlier features; as mentioned earlier, the references must involve a degree of simplification and regularization. For instance, László Somfai says of No. 5, the quartet referred to as 'The Dream' on account of its slow movement: 'most of the material of the finale paraphrases the Dream-Adagio (while listening to it one first of all recalls the lulling chord-pendulum)'.[3] What is significant for our purposes is that the 'chord-pendulum', presented in an almost atemporal context in the Adagio, is now regularly ordered within the metrical confines of a lively 6/8 time. A quite different application of the same principle can be found toward the end of the finale of No. 1. Taking as its point of reference the compositional problem of the first movement – beginning with a closing gesture and the subsequent attempts to place this in the correct syntactic context – the finale regularizes this to the point of parody. It presents so many strong closing gestures as to constitute a pun on the nature and role of a last movement, as Haydn seems to be asking 'How final must a finale be?'

For all that the finales of Op. 50 are animated on different levels by the spirit of the sonata style, it may be argued that the minuets and trios are even more emblematic of the absorption of this principle into all parts of the cycle. The 'Scherzo' designation of Op. 33 is cast off, and the movements are consistently put in third place. This should not, however, imply some sort of conservative retreat; in his quartets, unlike the symphonies with their more public face, Haydn was under no compulsion to write minuets that were even theoretically danceable to. In the current set, though, the incidence of what Keller calls 'anti-minuets'[4] is particularly high, not just in terms of their rhythmic irregularities but also the intellectualism of their procedures. Moreover, the trios only accentuate this trend. Instead of the customary more or less independent interlude, they present a continuation of the musical processes set in train by the minuet. This is most obvious in the trios of Nos. 4 and 5. Indeed, as we have seen, that of the F major quartet begins with exactly the same material as the preceding minuet; in No. 4 the head-motive from the minuet is treated polyphonically. A clear parallel can be drawn with the central instability and more intensive treatment of material in the sonata-form development section. The trio of No. 6 also marks a stage of intensification. Its material relationship to the minuet might not seem to be particularly close, but one only need consider the respective opening phrases in the first violin: both emphasize a repeated a^2 before leading to a third-beat *sforzando* tied over the bar, followed by scalic descent. Exceptionally, the trio is also much longer than its companion minuet; this is primarily the result of an engaging tentativeness in its sense of direction, so much at odds with the swagger of the minuet.

In a sense, the trio of No. 6 marks a half-way point between the trios of Nos. 4 and 5 and those of the first three quartets. While its sense of musical process renders it more unstable than the minuet, the material by which this is achieved is more relaxed. As such, it reminds us of the more traditional role of this middle section. We expect trios to lower the level of tension through tunefulness, regular phrase-lengths, simple textures, harmonic stability and a more indulgent use of instrumental colour. No doubt Haydn sensed that this was inappropriate to the technical mood of the set; given the challenging nature of the minuets, to have allowed the trios their customary role of relaxation would have been to evade the issue. Yet the trios of Nos. 1, 2, and 3 seem to fulfil these expectations; they appear to have the same rustic flavour as, for instance, the trios of Op. 33 Nos. 2 and 3. All have first sections of a squareness and simplicity that promise a larger retreat from the activity of the minuets. However, all three find ways of going awry after the double bar and reflecting back on their minuets in the process. In No. 1 the prominent rising-semitone motive from the first phrase of the minuet (c), superimposed with the ♩ |♪♪♪ |♪ rhythm of that phrase and its staccato repeated notes, is heard twice in the first period of the trio (see Example 6).

Thus this trio can be said to represent a continuation of the argument of the minuet, but by inverting its musical procedures. Its contrasting nature must be understood in a quite different sense to that provided by the traditional trio, in which the contrasts are self-evident and unforced: in the Op. 50 movement the differences have a specific larger purpose. Indeed, all the third movements of Op. 50 share this formal self-consciousness. Without exception they are concerned with matters of dominant preparation and structural return, almost to the point of being a fetish. This internal consistency within the set is indicative of the extent to which the functional origins of the dance form have been left behind. While the majority of Haydn's minuets have a purpose beyond that of presenting a stylized version of the dance, they rarely take so consistently extreme a position as do the minuets of Op. 50. Only Nos. 1 and 4 preserve to an extent the tone and gestures of the courtly minuet. As a group, though, the movements are informed by a new toughness of vision. The most important consequence of this is that the minuet and trio has now become, on its own terms, an intellectual and technical match for the first movement. Just as the trios of Op. 50 have become absorbed into a larger-scale process, so the minuet movements as a whole now demonstrate their relevance to a more intensive brand of musical discourse.

This greater intensity could, however, be problematical from the point of view of the Classical style. The need to resolve fully and explicitly means that every point of tension must be balanced by a point of release. Thus the idea of writing a multi-movement work in which each movement is of equal intensity and weight was not a possibility for the style. The role of the minuets in Op. 50 might therefore have presented difficulties if there were no compensation elsewhere in the structure. However, their traditional relaxing role has to an extent been transferred to the slow movements of the set. This shift in balance might anyway be deduced from the fact that for the first time in a set of quartets Haydn consistently puts the slow movement in second place. It is now in a position to provide an immediate release after the rigour of the first movement; it is no accident that Rosen highlights the combination of 'a lyrical breadth and a tranquil gravity rare in Haydn until now'.[6] Also relevant to this understanding is the variety apparent in the composer's large-scale formal approach. Although all are based on either variation or sonata principles, each of the slow movements yields a quite distinct formal scheme. Thus within the variation-based movements we hear a straightforward strophic set (No. 1), a set of double variations (No. 4), and in No. 3 an ambiguous

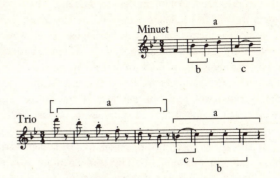

Example 6 Op. 50 No. 1, movement III

After the double bar it is then treated to a sort of stretto that destroys the effect of the bar lines. This undercuts the metrical regularity with which the trio's opening section had presented itself, and its return in the second part is now preceded by what sounds like six successive upbeats from bars 54 to 56. Not surprisingly, the earlier confidence is rather undermined, and the descending arpeggio is now presented in a type of hocket between the two violins, as if there are now different opinions as to where the downbeat should fall.

The trio of No. 3, like a number of the others, begins with a direct reference to the opening gambit of the minuet (see Example 7).

Example 7 Op. 50 No. 3, movement III

Unlike that section, however, which constructed itself entirely out of the initial unit in exemplary 'monothematic' manner, the trio becomes more interested in its own accompaniment than in the tune. The pursual of this pattern causes the middle section to overshoot itself by four bars; we clearly expect a return of the theme from the last beat of bar 73. However, it seems that this obligation has been forgotten in the fascination with the accompaniment; its hypnotic alternations of bowed pairs and staccato notes derive of course from the minuet itself, so that in a sense the monothematicism is simply transferred to a different level of the texture. The delay in the return of the trio theme as the cello pursues the quaver pattern for four further bars – the first and only time this instrument has a chance to play it – means that its reappearance functions more as a coda than as a structural reprise at the right point of the form. This understanding is reinforced by the way the first violin replaces the expected equivalent of bar 63 by continuous quavers in the third-to-last bar.

In the C major Quartet the trio also begins with a reference to the minuet's opening and dominating phrase. The falling arpeggio is here reversed and given the foil of a quaver accompaniment, as in No. 3; but whereas in that section the opening unit was somewhat liquidated during the course of the music, the trio of No. 2 uses the arpeggiated rhythmic cell throughout. In this respect it simply continues the procedure of the minuet, but on a more concentrated level. While in the minuet every phrase had begun with this rhythmic cell, the trio seems to telescope this procedure, as if giving a summary of the minuet's melodic action. In spite of such procedural and thematic links, and perhaps also because of them, the trio sounds very remote from the world of the minuet. As such, it serves as a good example of the heightened combination of rigour and freedom in the whole set. Precisely because some elements of the argument are fixed, the free or varied aspects emerge with greater impact. In fact the trio of No. 2 can be understood as a parody of its minuet, not just in terms of guying its melodic construction, but also in a wider stylistic sense. The movement as a whole revives the stylistic dualism of the opening Vivace, which juxtaposed the learned and the light. Here the innocuous-sounding trio is framed by a serious and effortful minuet. The trios of Nos. 1 and 3 share this element of stylistic parody.

There is another, more specific sense in which the trio of No. 2 takes issue with the minuet and provides a reverse image to it. The matter of harmonic propriety is taken up by David Wyn Jones:

The Menuet extends the usual three stages of its structure – theme to double bar, development and restatement – to four by adding an eighteen-bar coda. The reason for this extension is to be found in the tonal course charted by the movement. The texture is completely free of padding, each phrase beginning with a [...] joined by chromatic harmony to articulate a cadence; the cadence at the [...] is in C major. After the double bar the music moves to D minor and [...] harmonic and rhythmic cul-de-sac at bars 18 and 19. Another five bars [...] lead directly into the repetition of the main theme in C major. Thus, in [...] movement, the only other key which has been established is D min[...] absence of any preparation for the return of the tonic makes the reprise o[...] an unsettled one. What Haydn does, in effect, is to have a double repri[...] concluding with an interrupted cadence, the second (led by the violin) [...] being heard over a dominant pedal in order to secure C major. The tr[...] avoids formal conventions but with an added touch of humour ... Afte[...] bar, as if to emphasize the lack of tonal preparation in the minuet, the m[...] securely on a dominant chord. But beware; when Haydn is apparently [...] naive he is often also at his most resourceful, and here – instead of [...] reprise – there is a new, farcical chain of events, two false starts (one *fo*[...] *piano*), a silent bar, a third beginning led by the cello, and, finally, [...] 'reprise', except that the dialogue is now heard above a stepwise as[...] rather than descending. Whereas the minuet had dealt with the proble[...] insecure reprise, the trio does the opposite, overcoming a preparation [...] secure.[5]

Indeed, on a higher level, the trio also makes up for th[...] over-ambition of the minuet. Thus the movement to V at the c[...] comparatively unemphatic, and after this point F♯ is immediat[...] by F♮ (bar 59); in other words, not only is there now too mu[...] ation', but it all takes place firmly within the orbit of C major. V[...] the dominant, but we are never firmly *in* it. This explains the [...] at the point of reprise. Haydn, once more conscience-stricke[...] 'ineptitude', realizes that there is no justification for a return [...] If the movement away from the tonic key has been negl[...] structural reprise has no function. Without an appropria[...] harmonic tension since the first appearance of the theme, [...] lation has nothing to reinforce. It is therefore doubly ir[...] 'reprise' in the last eight bars features the only real chromatic [...] the trio. These act as an internal adjustment within the trio [...] as a preparation for the return of the minuet, with its [...] harmonic language. The cello line makes this function mo[...] C♯–D of 76–7 and F–F♯–G–C at bars 79–82 will be hear[...] first section of the repeated minuet (bars 2 and 7–8). A [...] reversal can be heard in the fact that the trio is most comple[...] at the same point at which the minuet is attempting to resolv[...]

blend of ternary, rondo, and variation principles that will be investigated later.

Again, however, this variety does not just amount to a contrast in musical thought; each slow movement responds to the preceding first movement in an appropriate and necessarily different way. Thus in Nos. 1 and 2 very fully argued sonata-form movements are followed by slow movements that have something of the character of an interlude or intermezzo. Yet no two slow movements could be more distinct from one another. No. 1 follows the most obviously monothematic Allegro of the opus with a concentrated set of variations on a single theme. The same constant reference to a single gesture that sustained the first movement is also present here and is now also, of course, built into the form. In spite of the procedural similarities, however, the slow movement offers a radically different sense of musical flow: in place of the trochaic units that were reiterated in the Allegro, the iambic shape of its melodic lines generates, as Hans Keller has noted, a strong feeling of repose.[7] This is all the more striking since Haydn marks the movement 'Adagio' rather than the Andante which the 6/8 time-signature and accompanimental rhythms might lead one to expect.

The slow movement of No. 2, on the other hand, succeeds a 3/4 Vivace with pronounced internal contrasts and moves in the direction of greater metrical and rhythmic squareness. It, too, evinces some similarities of procedure to its opening movement. Both begin with a double statement of their first long paragraph, and, just as the Vivace contained the only conventional second subject of any of the first movements, so the slow movement features a distinctively new tune at bars 22ff. Although this clearly refers to the turn figure exposed at the beginning of the movement, it is placed in a quite different context – rhythmically, since the very regular quaver accompaniment has disappeared for the first time, and texturally, since the homophonic style has been turned on its head. Whereas previously there were three accompanying instruments and one solo, now the first violin sustains an upper-voice pedal note while the others all take part in the presentation of the new material. The second subject of the first movement was also distinguished primarily by its textural and rhythmic shape rather than simply being a 'new tune'.

On a different level, this movement also continues the stylistic duality of the first but concentrates the Vivace's ambiguity of tone. Whereas the first movement juxtaposed learned and light styles (compare for instance the fugato that starts the development with the chattering second subject), the

Adagio fuses the two registers. This ambiguity can be appreciated by noting the diversity of critical reaction to the movement. Jones comments:

Profundity is certainly the last word to describe [this] slow movement, which emerges as a parody of a serenade. Thirty years earlier, Haydn would have disdained the plodding accompaniments and the short-breathed phrases. Here, fortified by the experience of writing slow operatic arias, they produce an ironic interlude in the middle of so much cerebration.[8]

Somfai also refuses to take the movement at face value:

The [second] movement also balances on the verge of the banal and the eccentric: seemingly a real *cantabile* violin solo with the usual staccato chordal accompaniment, it is interspersed with such overstrung gestures and poses as to seem almost ironical.[9]

On the other hand Günter Thomas describes the movement as being 'emotionally charged',[10] and, judging from the absence of words to the contrary, other writers such as Keller presumably feel the same way.

The issue is not one of correct interpretation; ultimately one can come down firmly on neither side, since both genuine feeling and the element of parody play their part in the make-up of the movement. As such the movement is a fine illustration of the concept of *tone* in the Classical style. This has to do with the relationship of the composer to his material or musical 'characters' and implies a balance in his attitude between detachment and belief.[11] Thus Haydn carries out his plan in this Adagio with both conviction in the emotional effectiveness of his material and a regard for the slightly shopworn means of expression. This can be heard clearly in the coda, whose sentimental farewelling devices – the pointedly 'expressive' chromatic degrees in the bass line, the interrupted cadence at bars 56–7, the 'pathetic' embroidery in the first violin at bar 58 – are both amusing and moving. Above all this, though, the Adagio proceeds directly and consistently from the double-edged nature of the first movement. Likewise, and once again for all the difference of musical effect, the slow movement of No. 1 reinterprets the purity and asceticism of language of its preceding Allegro.

The other slow movements of the set respond to different circumstances while at the same time also providing an element of release. Those of Nos. 4 and 6 are, comparatively speaking, the most complex; in both cases this is conditioned by the fact that their first movements achieve a relatively weak sense of closure. Neither first movement ends with the sense of security that derives from a well-rounded musical argument, as presented in Nos. 1 and 2. Indeed, in both works Haydn is particularly interested in developing a cumulative argument through movements of relatively equal complexity, and this leads to the two most distinctive finales of the opus – as observed earlier, the only two not to contain rondo elements in their construction.

On the other hand, Nos. 3 and 5 contain the lightest outer movements of the set, and in each case the slow movement represents the heart of the work. That of No. 3 is in the dominant key, Bb major, a much rarer choice than the usual subdominant. Its effect, of course, is to throw the movement into relief against its companions. Haydn often chose the dominant when he had something special to say: witness the slow movements of Symphonies Nos. 88 and 98 or the Quartet, Op. 76 No. 3, whose second movement is the well-known set of variations on Haydn's Imperial hymn, 'Gott erhalte Franz den Kaiser'. A more extreme example of the principle of sharp-side emphasis to the same expressive end is found in the F♯ major Largo e mesto of the D major Quartet, Op. 76 No. 5. However, while the Bb major slow movement of Op. 50 No. 3 is tonally tense in relation to the first movement, rhythmically it is more relaxed. Its profundity might easily be masked by the fact that this is the quickest of the set's slow movements, being marked 'Andante più tosto allegretto'. As such it has a sort of 'walking tread' that places it in a specialized sub-group of Haydn's output along with such slow movements as those of the 'Drumroll' Symphony, No. 103, and the Quartet, Op. 77 No. 2. All of these movements, adopting a similar brisk tempo in 2/4, begin with two-part writing and feature brief flurries of dotted rhythms. In addition, all are guided by a similar spirit, one of inexorable forward motion. In the case of Op. 50 No. 3 the stature of the piece can be heard not so much in the individual lines, which are not especially beautiful or remarkable, as in the power of movement they project. This power has a narrative quality that might perhaps be compared to the rhythms that drive the Chopin Ballades. Yet this Andante più tosto allegretto also represents a 'type' that was to be found in not-so-slow movements by other Classical composers, as in the second movements of Mozart's Piano Trio, K. 542, or Clementi's Piano Sonata, Op. 34 No. 1 (Example 8).

For all these comparisons, the movement loses none of its extraordinary character within its own quartet, described by Cecil Gray as 'curiously ethereal and disembodied'.[12] Its affinity with the preceding movement lies primarily at a deep structural level – both are decidedly ambiguous about their recapitulations, reversing the expected order of return and saving their major twist until near the end.

Example 8 Clementi Op. 34 No. 1, movement II

The slow movement of No. 5, cast in the more usual subdominant key, also manages to be both a highlight and a point of repose within its quartet. On the surface it might appear to be, along with No. 2, texturally the most old-fashioned of the Op. 50 slow movements. However, just as No. 2 managed to subvert its soprano aria associations, the present slow movement goes well beyond a basis of tune and accompaniment. For a start, there is no tune in any conventional sense, rather a series of stray melodic impulses. The only recognizable melodic units are the bits of standard Classical phraseology used to denote phrase-endings. One of these is heard in the first violin at bars 3–4 (and repeated at 24–5); the other, more important unit, occurs in near-identical form at bars 7–8, 18–19, and 43–4, and at 28 and 38, where it is strategically cut short. Much of the expressive effect of the movement comes rather from the 'accompanying' parts, which move in waves of parallel chordal motion, like a sort of Classical organum. These produce a strangely uninsistent sort of tension against the upper 'melodic' part, which several times intersects the parallel chords to move to the bottom of the texture. The resulting mood is fantastic and rhapsodic, although it can hardly be said to prefigure Romanticism. Rather, the mixture of warmth and a certain austerity makes a companion piece to some of Haydn's other late slow movements, such as those of Symphony No. 102 (also full of 'wandering' sextuplets) and Piano Trio No. 36.

A nearer temporal equivalent can be found in the slow movement of Symphony No. 86, entitled 'Capriccio'. This represents a type of slow movement almost unique to Haydn in that it is concerned with rhetoric rather than song. Haydn plays with fragments of the Classical language, its clichés in particular, as he seems to ruminate on their status as musical gestures.[13] It is also characteristic of the composer in this and the other slow movements mentioned that he achieves his greatest intensity of thought by a process of simplification rather than one of enrichment, as Mozart does. Thus for all the richness and ambiguity of the end-product, the means from which Haydn proceeds are remarkably and deliberately bare – a simple rising arpeggio in Symphony No. 86, a similar device in the like-minded Adagio of Symphony No. 68, or a restricted textural premise in Op. 50 No. 5. The investigative character that informs all these movements makes the present example something of an exception in terms of Op. 50. There is an element of it in No. 3 as well, but, as has been mentioned, this is only possible because the outer movements of both works are comparatively concise and lightweight.

Taken as a group, the slow movements of Op. 50 are not designed to challenge the listener or present an investigation into the state of the language, since this role of stylistic deliberation has passed to the third movements. Nevertheless, in their own capacities they maintain the approach apparent in the other movements of the opus. Compared with Op. 33, for instance, they are notably concentrated in their use of material: they are structured in a more reiterative and sectional fashion. Thus, in a manner consistent with their preceding first movements, they take their cue from a determination to be faithful to creative 'first thoughts'.

8

The individual works

No. 1 in B♭ major

Many accounts of Op. 50 have begun by commenting on the two bars of repeated B♭s for cello that begin the whole set. These are generally taken to be either a compliment to the cello-playing dedicatee of the set, or, as Rosen says in view of the extreme simplicity of this 'solo', a 'charming joke'.[1] On a larger scale, much has been made of the nature of the cello part, a perspective challenged by Somfai:

> With Haydn's Prussian Quartets it has ... become commonplace to refer to the 'royal' cello part, although there is no proper basis for this. To have the instrument play the theme in the slow movement of the E flat major quartet, or to have the cello take over the leading part at the repetition of the theme of the minuet in B flat major, had been normal occurrences in Haydn's string quartets since his Op. 20. Actually, the first two quartets (in B flat major and C major) were probably ready by the time the thought of a dedication emerged at all.[2]

Of course we can never know the precise chronology of Haydn's intentions with respect to the dedication, although Somfai's claim is supported by the surviving correspondence. It is still possible that Haydn had the Prussian monarch in mind from the very outset. In any case, surely the most significant part of the story is how little Haydn felt he needed to accommodate the works themselves to this fact. This tells us something about his perception of his status in the musical (and social) world; it is also temperamentally revealing. In the three quartets of 1789–90 that he dedicated to Friedrich Wilhelm, K. 575, 589, and 590, Mozart showed his desire to please and flatter in much more literal fashion. In these works the many tunes entrusted to the cello lead to a more concertante style of quartet writing, as the other instruments respond in kind. Haydn, by contrast, produced in Op. 50 perhaps his most hermetic set of quartets. The same trait is apparent when one considers another possible external influence on Op. 50, that of Mozart himself: Haydn seems to have responded by becoming more than ever his own master.

However, a more important feature that is present at the very beginning of the first quartet does suggest a fairly direct Mozartean influence; indeed, according to Landon, it is 'the one direct influence we may trace to Haydn's study of Mozart's six quartets (those dedicated to Haydn)'. This is the fact that Haydn 'has adopted an entirely new system of tempo', involving the 'halving of the old eight-eight pace into barred C'.[3] Whereas at the time of Op. 17, for instance, Haydn would have felt the pulse in terms of four per bar, involving quite elaborate subdivisions of each beat, there is now an increasing sense of movement by the whole or half-bar. The semiquavers and demisemiquavers that filled out many beats in the 'old system' are replaced by a 'base rate' of triplet quavers in the present movement; the semiquavers that are present invariably form part of a written-out and rhythmicized turn. The end result is that the music seems to move more quickly and lightly, and the sense of phrase is expanded. Significantly, Haydn now simply writes 'Allegro' at the head of the movement. An old-style comparison can in fact be drawn within the confines of Op. 50: the first movement of No. 5, marked Allegro moderato and in 2/4 time, features a 'base rate' of triplet semiquavers and is described by Isidor Saslav as a 'last farewell to the previous style'.[4]

It is not just for these reasons that the first movement of No. 1 has received particularly close critical attention. It represents an extreme in 'monothematic' writing that is remote from our usual perceptions of late eighteenth-century style. The fact that Beethoven clearly echoes the opening gesture in his first published string quartet, Op. 18 No. 1 (see Example 9), testifies to the impact that Haydn's movement must have made on him. However, it also emphasizes the wide gulf between the two movements. Beethoven seems to have largely replicated the monothematic surface of the Haydn movement without realizing the justification for the older composer's thematic economy. It has already been argued that in the first movements of Op. 50 the monothematicism as such is not of primary importance; in every case Haydn starts from an 'improper assumption' that requires his full attention if the irregularity is to be resolved. Haydn's opening is placed in a context of impropriety while Beethoven's opening is a determined statement of unity.

That the first movement of No. 1 should have set the tone for the received critical opinion on Op. 50 is further testimony to its exceptional brand of musical argument. Its procedures are more extreme than those

Example 9 Beethoven Op. 18 No. 1, movement I

of the other opening movements only because it starts with a more ticklish problem – a closing cadential gesture. Number 6 also begins with a cadential formula, but one that is smaller-scale and less disruptive. (Its consequences for the whole work are, however, just as far-reaching.) The other opening movements differ in method but not in kind: in No. 3, as we have seen, the 'theme' is over by the second bar, while in No. 4 the theme does not really reach an end. All the movements question Classical proprieties, whether their opening units start at the wrong juncture, finish too early, or do not finish at all. These themes pose a linguistic challenge: Haydn states *x*, then asks 'What is wrong with statement *x*?'. The answering of the question constitutes the rest of the movement.

The cadential formula that begins Op. 50 No. 1 has been treated to an extensive analysis by Janet M. Levy. Through conventional association, she argues, this formula functions as an archetypal closing gesture. By way of comparison she cites the closing bars of Symphony No. 89, also written in 1787 (Example 10): this passage

has not previously been heard in the movement. Haydn can, nonetheless, be sure that his audience will understand its function, because it is drawn from the common stock of conventional closing gestures for movements; precisely because the new material is stereotyped it does not disturb the listener's sense of coherence.

68

Example 10 Haydn Symphony No. 89, movement IV

Our quartet opening has a similar patterning to the Symphony, with the 'implication ... that what follows "should be" precisely analogous to mm. 202–03'.

However, because Haydn's continuation in Op. 50 No. 1 does not lead to the tonic scale-degree – rather he transposes the gesture up a third at bars 5–6 – the closing function of the passage is undermined. This forms

the first in a long series of postponements and playful distortions of the 'proper' continuation of the gesture. The rhetoric of the movement is partly dependent on the fact that the strongly implied closing gesture is not merely an indivisible cadential figure ... but, in its archetypal form, consists of two parts, the first of which (mm. 3–4) clearly implies the second. Indeed, the whole movement can be conceived of as a subtle play on ways of avoiding the conventional conjunction of the second phrase of the closing gesture with the first phrase, [meaning an] avoidance of the complete gesture ... until it occurs in the appropriate formal context, the very close of the movement.

Levy examines most of the subsequent occurrences of the gesture until the 'proper' form is presented 'with utter syntactic propriety' in the coda (from bar 150). For the first time the tonic pedal is retained through the whole unit, before the phrase is unexpectedly expanded to yield a still richer sense of closure (bars 156–9). She also notes the ambiguity surrounding the exact point of recapitulation.[5] It seems to occur at a 'mid-way point' of the original theme, at about bar 110. It is of course in Haydn's interest to underplay the area of reprise so as not to undermine the effect of the coda.

The reader is also directed to Rosen's account of this movement. He too finds great richness, in spite of the supposedly austere monothematic surface, by focussing on another aspect of the material, the Eb–D pair heard at the start in the first violin (bars 3–4).[6] In conjunction Rosen's and Levy's accounts bring home the remarkable fusion of contrast and unity so characteristic of Haydn in his economical mode; because the material Haydn uses is so precisely heard and understood in all its implications, it is the variety of its settings that strikes one most forcibly. Indeed, for Leonard Ratner the Eb–D illustrates the use of species-contrapuntal technique in Haydn: as the principal 'motive' of the movement it can be 'placed in any kind of harmonic context'. (Rosen points out that the Eb is present in every dissonant chord for the first fifteen bars.) Ratner comments that it is 'typical of Haydn to take a tired figure of this sort and make it come alive'.[7]

On the surface the freest part of the movement is the recapitulation, but its freedom has a specific purpose. Functioning as a paraphrase rather than a true reprise of expository material, its task is to reaffirm the tonic key without detracting from the events of the coda. Thus, after the ambiguous point of return, it completely avoids the six-note figure that was so prevalent at the start of the exposition and in the development section. More crucially, it ignores the crotchet pedal motive, not just in terms of its rhythmic shape (with the minor exceptions of bars 127 and 142–3, in the *upper voices*) but also in terms of its tonic pitch. Indeed, a bass Bb is almost completely avoided. In particular, on the first beats of bars 134, 140, and 147, where each time we are led to expect a Bb in the cello, Haydn finds alternative means of continuation. This means that in harmonic and large-scale rhythmic terms the whole recapitulation ultimately functions as an extended upbeat to the return of the Bb bass crotchet pedal at bar 150. Thus Haydn saves all his true recapitulation, in the sense of resolution, until the coda, an exceptional state of affairs. Indeed, much of the nominal recapitulation sounds like a cadenza or a fantasy on the previous material, especially when the F is held for five bars by the cello at bars 132–6. This makes the longer-held Bb pedal of the coda a logical answer to the F. Haydn goes one step further in the last few bars and unifies the tonic pedal with the triplet rhythm that had dominated the reprise. The emphasis on the coda as a means of resolution rather than just reaffirmation is found elsewhere in Op. 50: the first movements of Nos. 3 and 5 contain codas of similar weight and intent.

Hans Keller has made the imaginative suggestion that the opening material of the movement – repeated notes alone in the cello with the subsequent addition of dissonant upper voices – might be indebted to the beginning of Mozart's 'Dissonance' Quartet, K. 465. However plausible the matter of influence may be in this instance, the different continuations by the two composers – as with Beethoven's Op. 18 No. 1, which builds on the Haydn – are even more revealing. The most important aspect of the comparison concerns listening technique: how the listener is to approach Haydn's more rigorous structure. Somfai has discussed this matter with regard to Op. 33, but his words are at least as relevant to Op. 50:

But we can rightfully say that today's audience, taking part at the customary concert forms of today, often … listen to the masterpieces of Haydn's Op. 33 from the wrong point of view, and indeed, it is difficult for the listener to cope with the music's own characteristic wave-lengths. True, the rigorous dialectics in the composition, the 'speed' of changes of musical textures and events, and the ideal of symmetry and balance of Op. 33 strongly deviate from any chamber music written during the Beethoven-Brahms century; it is so much more fluent, so much more condensed and restless that it is closer, practically speaking, to … 20th century chamber music, than to the Viennese classical and romantic generations following him. Because of the fast speed of events, Haydn quartets are not vertically 'dense' (like, for example, the synchronous contrapuntal or rhythmical complexities of Beethoven or Brahms), but rather horizontally 'dense' in their rapid rhythmic and motivic successions, in the refined network of motives which refer to one another … Therefore, if one begins listening to the music of Op. 33 with an intellectual time-table and distribution of energy in preparation for … 8[-] or 16-measured melodic phrases or the spacious Beethoven themes, one will inevitably miss out on the happenings – at least in the opening movements.[8]

As Somfai would seem to imply, one might expect a slow movement to be less challenging for the listener. However, the Adagio of Op. 50 No. 1 contains several features that might also by-pass a present-day audience. The first variation features a fine example of the conversational textures that are so underappreciated in the Haydn quartets (the opening of Op. 50 No. 3 has already been examined in this respect). Here there is drama and wit in a context that would seem to allow neither. The second violin takes over the tune in its literal form from the last quaver of bar 12. In bar 14 the first violin imitates the second, at a half-bar's distance but without a *fz* on the A♮. In the following bar the first violin, perhaps anxious to reclaim the melodic leadership, tries to smother the second with a rising demisemi-quaver run; this has no effect, as the second violin continues steadily along its chosen melodic route. With this ploy unsuccessful, the first returns to its previous turn figure, which it repeats in isolated form three times. The tone has changed, however. What was in bar 14 a nod of agreement has now entered into competition with the tune. This reiteration acts as a spoiling tactic, and in bar 18 violin II relents. It joins with the first an octave lower.

However, the second violin regains the initiative after the double bar. It reverts for two bars to the literal form of the theme while the first violin plays once more its rising scale figure. Then, from the end of bar 20, it finally introduces some variation of the theme. The eloquence of these variations seems to silence the first violin; ironically, they are achieved by means of the turn figure with which it had tried to assert itself. First of all the rhythm of the turn figure is incorporated in the descending line at 20–1, then in the two melodic units at 22–3 its contour is suggested. Indeed, the whole shape here assumes the likeness of the cell at 1^6–2^2, with the simplified turn figure followed by an expressive downward leap. This is a good example of a variation that does not so much distance or take us away from the theme as bring us closer. In other words, the variation provides a more unified statement than the theme itself. The varied form of the original solitary G♭ from bar 11, at the end of bar 23, also reworks the turn figure to confirm the melodic control that the second violin has achieved.

The presence of the G♭ itself provides another feature that demands the active understanding of the listener. This note, leaving a sting at the end of a restful theme, looks both back and forward. It is a strongly pointed reminder of the dissonant F♯/G♭ that counterpointed the E♭ in the first movement. This was the first chromatic note to be introduced in the Allegro, at bar 9^4. Haydn often utilizes the immediate aural impact of such a note at turning-points in the subsequent harmonic structure. In this case the note is heard prominently at bars 14 and 16, and especially at 28 within the first few paragraphs of the Allegro. In addition, the G♭ anticipates the tonic minor of the Adagio's second variation, where the first violin has regained the melodic leadership and the other instruments play a distinctly Schubertian type of accompaniment. However, in its immediate melodic context the Gb of the Adagio theme does not resolve, as it should, by step in the same register. This resolution must wait until the coda. After a literal repetition of the closing bars of the theme at 56^6–8^4, the final unit is repeated by the second violin while the first provides a gentle decoration. At 59^4 violin I reaches a g(♮)^1 so that the flattened third scale degree just heard at 57^6 is finally 'corrected' with respect to the tonic key of Eb major. This 'purification' is reinforced by the final melodic motion of the movement, with the first violin's simple fall from g^1 to eb^1.

There is another sense in which the coda attempts to untie the knot created at the end of the original theme. Not only did the non-resolving Gb create an unsatisfying effect but the closure of the theme altogether was rather constricted in its expression, particularly given the long-breathed phrases that preceded it. In the coda therefore (from bar 47^6) Haydn simply provides a large expansion of the theme's last two phrases (bars 8^6–12^4). Significantly, he begins with a recollection of the second violin's first-variation shape from bars 20^6–1. The original phrase of 8^6–10 is then subjected to still more intensification at bars 50^6–2. The viola, the only instrument not to feature soloistically thus far, plays a swirling figure at this most poignant part of the movement, like a brief cadenza. The intervallic pattern it forms with the first violin each half-bar of tritone or fifth resolving inwards to the third (tenth), in conjunction with the Bb pedal in the cello, suggests a heightened form of the material that began the Allegro (at bars 3–4, where Eb–A resolves to D–Bb over a Bb bass).

This transformation is so memorable that Haydn recalls it – unconsciously, no doubt – in the finale. At bars 117–22 of the Vivace assai the first violin recalls its bars 51–2 of the Adagio. In both passages the second violin plays precisely the same progression, c^2–bb^1–ab^1–g^1, with more animated note values lower in the texture. Both sections finish with a quick descending scale in the first violin (bar 53 of the slow movement, bar 123 of the finale). In the Adagio this scale leads to a fierce *forte* unison of all four instruments at bar 54. This forms a different sort of textural climax to go with the widely-spaced sound of the previous few bars, but the unison has been prepared by brief passages beforehand – the rhythmic unisons of bars 37 and 39, and the striking decoration of the disruptive Gb at bar 46. Following this, Haydn expands the final phrase of the theme in the manner previously described. Here then is another coda that makes up for what has been missing in the earlier material.

The theme of this variation movement has also had the distinction of having been set to words. In 1793 Count Harrach, the Lord of Rohrau, had erected a pyramid-shaped monument in honour of Rohrau's most famous son (Haydn was born there). On two sides of the pyramid were inscribed verses by the poet Gabriele von Baumberg, one to the slow movement of Symphony No. 53 and the other to the present movement.[9]

The theme of the minuet presents a condensed version of the slow movement theme. Rising arpeggio with upbeat beginning followed by rising semitone from A♮ to B♭, at 0^3–2^2, parallel the opening unit of the Adagio, the earlier *fz* on the A now matched by a downbeat placement at 2^1. The two-bar unit is then repeated at a higher pitch, also as in the Adagio. The following descending 6/3 chords at bars 4^3–6^3 then suggest the progression of bars 8^6–10 of the Adagio, both beginning with the same three pitches – eb^2, bb^1, and g^1. (A more precise melodic parallel to this Adagio passage emerges later in the minuet, where at 21^3–4^2 the first violin plays three pairs of descending diatonic steps in the same syncopated rhythm.) The twofold reiteration of an opening unit, the second occurrence higher in pitch than the first, reminds us that the first movement also began in this manner. Quite apart from any motivic interconnections, this forms an important procedural link between the first three movements.

The minuet can also be linked more directly with the Allegro – the two tritone-plus-resolution intervallic pairs at bars 2 and 4 (for instance the A–E♭ to B♭–D in first violin and cello at bar 2) form a familiar pattern. When this unit is given its most stable harmonization at bars 32^3–4^2 of the brief 'coda', the B♭ pedal in the cello and the gb^1–f^1 fall in the second violin provide further links with the first movement (compare, for instance, bars 14–15 of the Allegro).

The trio in turn contains both motivic and procedural links to the minuet. It too begins with a phrase that is then repeated in transposed form. This time, however, the repetition moves downward in pitch, and the whole unit now covers a section. The principle of thematic construction that has governed all the themes of the quartet thus far is expanded here into an antecedent-consequent phrase-structure. In motivic terms, the trio distils the minuet's two main building-blocks, the rising arpeggio (here inverted) and the semitone step (see Example 6). Indeed, the trio's reinterpretation of minuet shapes continues beyond the double bar. Just as its first period reworks the first four bars of the minuet, so the continuation inverts and fragments the falling chromatic fourths of bars 4^3–6 (the inversion having already been accomplished in more straightforward manner by the second violin, in the minuet's last two bars). As described earlier, this results in a stretto effect, one that replaces the coordinated three-voice performance of the shape in the minuet with a sense of squabbling disagreement. The effect is all the more striking after the unanimity of the shape's immediate model, the units at bars 38^3–40^1 and 42^3–4^1. (These in turn form an echo of the unexpected unison phrase-endings at bars 37 and 39 of the slow movement; the connection is strengthened by the common articulation of slurred pair followed by staccato repeated notes.) It is perhaps hardly surprising that the players should come unstuck after the double bar; the exaggerated simplicity of rhythm and texture in the first period seems all too cosy after the fluidity of the minuet.

The climax of the disagreements comes at bars 50^3–1^1, where the communication between the players reaches its lowest ebb. The clashing g^2 and ab^2 between the two violins seems to represent a verticalization of the horizontal semitone pairs that have been prominent throughout the quartet. Another large-scale chromatic detail is found in the reappearance of $f\sharp^1$ in the viola at 44^3, initiating the pattern of staggered chromatic ascents. The $f\sharp^1$–g^1 returns in the viola at 58^3–9^1 to give a further twist to the trio's reprise.

The finale forms a parody of the first movement on two levels. As mentioned before, the movement plays on the idea of closure that animated the Allegro. Part of this strategy includes the insertion, as Hans Keller has pointed out, of two false recapitulations in the development section. The first, in the tonic key (!), is prepared by a marked rhythmic deceleration in all parts, long-held pedal notes, and the sentimental expectancy of a first violin part that sighs repeatedly (102–7) before embarking upon a brief cadenza at bar 108. All these features produce the effect of what Keller calls an 'ineluctable lead-back'; but 'Haydn's masterly escape route represents the very height of purely musical comedy'. The composer moves swiftly to an imitative passage which contains the reminiscence of the Adagio coda at bars 117ff. Before that, however, there is an equally striking echo of earlier material. The first violin's bb^2–a^2–ab^2–g^2 succession at 112–15, with the first crotchet bb^2 tied over the bar, recalls the same instrument's line at bars 28^3–30^1 of the minuet. It is not simply the identity of pitch and rhythm that makes this a strong connection: as so often in matters of thematic relationship, it is the sense of proportion, the structural placement of the recollection that counts. In both these passages the first violin line occurs four bars in from a point of reprise – one a real, one a false one. In the case of the following Adagio reminiscence, both passages are found in the middle of a larger phrase. Thus these interconnections are strengthened by their similar function in the given musical context.

Soon after this point a second false reprise is heard in the subdominant at bar 133. If Haydn has thereby doubly fooled us about the moment of true structural return, which finally ensues at bar 164 after a pointedly laboured preparation (156–63), he then does his best to avoid a finish to the work. 'Just as Haydn had started the work before the beginning', says Keller in view of the cello's 'accompaniment to nothing' in the Allegro, 'he pretends to finish it after the end'. After the 'false conclusion' at bar 222, which is 'not really quite final enough', we hear two bars of silence. Then the whole theme is heard again, preceded by the upbeat phrase played by the second violin at bars 8 and 171 but not previously heard on initial entry of the theme. This has a delightfully insouciant effect. Keller notes that, together with the tonic false reprise, this return of the theme gives a 'rondo tinge' to the movement, a structure implied already by the character of the theme. The restatement of the theme then 'forces the coda to produce its own coda, with three further false conclusions'.[10] These occur at bars 237, 241, and 243, making a total of five closures. 'When is enough enough?' Haydn seems to ask. This speculative game is ended by the intervention of the cello, whose rushing upward scale at 244 recalls its quick ascents in the second variation of the Adagio (bars 36ff).

The second level of parody of the first movement is more directly conceived. The endless reiterations of the same rhythmic figure recall the same feature in the Allegro. Again this has a motivic as well as a procedural basis. The rhythm heard time and again in the Finale – ♩ ♫ | (♩) – is a simplified version of the Allegro's ♩ ♫♫ ♫ | ♩, with the turn removed to the following part of the theme. The initial duration is contracted, but the trochaic emphasis remains. Finally it should be pointed out that the 'endless coda' has an internal logic within the finale itself. After the full close at bar 16 the exposition is marked by its great continuity; all subsequent material seems to be transitional in character. There is a lack of sufficient structural articulation and thematic stability, as every potential point of relaxation is denied. This avoidance of a large-scale structural downbeat, which naturally continues through the development in spite of its deceptive returns, necessitates a whole series of them at the end – in the form of emphatic full closes.

No. 2 in C major

The power of a theme in shaping the course of a movement and indeed a work has already become apparent in the examination of Op. 50. In terms of character, style, and technique the first material we hear can imply and make logical much of what is to follow. The stylistic dualism of the C major Quartet has been considered earlier: the ambiguity of the Adagio and the contrasting parts of the third movement issue from the juxtaposition of learned and lighter elements in the first movement. Not only does the first movement express these disjunctions on a large scale – the relaxed second subject (bars 43ff.) versus the warmth of the harmonic digression at 65–83 versus the soberly contrapuntal passages – but the conflict is already packed into the opening theme. Thus the first violin's line, angular and nervous but with a whiff of the contrapuntist's tag about it, stands at odds with the relaxed waltz-like accompaniment provided by the other instruments. Following this, at bars 10–11, Haydn once more almost seems to be putting words into his players' mouths. The sudden unison, *piano* and low in tessitura, seems to place a corporate question-mark after the rather desultory 'theme', asymmetrical and loosely presented. ('Did we really mean that?')

The unison also has the effect of undermining the strength of the preceding perfect cadence at bars 8–9. After this brief impasse a bold approach is adopted, with a *fz* secondary dominant chord to V, widely spaced after the preceding unison E. The players then move with a show of determination and virtuosity to the dominant, as if hoping that the movement may now proceed on a normal route to G major. However, the four emphatic chords of bars 17–18[1] are echoed uncertainly by a dominant seventh of the home key at 19–20[1], and the opening material then returns. It proceeds broadly as at the beginning, thus implying that it will act as a consequent to bars 1–20, which are momentarily understood as a very large antecedent phrase. Although the 'consequent' turns out to be a transition, this structural behaviour sets the terms for another important aspect of the movement and of the whole work. Unlike No. 1, with its obsessiveness and constant reiterations, No. 2 is a quartet that moves in broad and mostly well-defined paragraphs. It has already been pointed out that both first and second movements feature a clearly-defined area of thematic contrast in the manner of a second subject, an exceptional feature for this opus. The finale extends the consistency of this procedure by containing a thematically relaxed and texturally distinctive second theme. The definition of these themes is strengthened by the fact that they always recur verbatim, as if standing outside the transformations of material that occur elsewhere.

There are other respects in which the structural proportions of these three movements coincide. The syntactical character of the work is further

Example 11 Op. 50 No. 2

confirmed by the fact that the first movement, slow movement, and finale all begin with a double statement of their themes. In particular, the outer movements both feature counterstatements, beginning at bars 21 and 22 respectively, that turn into transitions via the use of a pivotal C♯ (of which more later). The resemblance actually involves shape as well as proportion (see Example 11): both counterstatements are preceded by a descending dominant arpeggio formed in groups of three (13ff./19–22) and a moment of suspense (silence/fermata).

Another common shaping that reinforces a common proportion lends the slow movement theme the aspect of a variation on the opening theme of the first movement. The closing shape of the Adagio theme at bars 7–8 is virtually identical to that in bars 7–9 of the Vivace. Both move from a sustained sixth scale-degree (a^2 in the Vivace, d^2 in the Adagio) through a scalic descent in equal rapid note values to a sustained tonic scale-degree (c^2/f^1). The subsequent elaborations of the cadence point are also very similar – appoggiatura on the third scale-degree leading to supertonic and tonic notes. What is more, the subsequent falling third at a lower pitch-level that had such a quizzical effect at bars 10–11 of the Vivace is replicated in the Adagio at bar 8, though now assuming a more conventional role of 'filler' before the repetition of the whole tune. The elaboration of this falling third by a dotted-rhythmic figure matches the form at 7^4 that also somewhat disguises the indebtedness to the Vivace model (see Example 12).

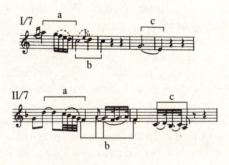

Example 12 Op. 50 No. 2

The f^1–a^1–g^1–f^1 shape at bars 7^3–8^1 that rounds off the Adagio theme can be heard as a retrograde of the f^1–g^1–a^1–f^1 with which the theme began (1–2^1), the dotted-rhythmic shape of bar 7^4 being a written-out form of the turn at bar 1^4. Indeed, the turn figure itself which plays such an important part in the whole Adagio (see, for instance, its accelerated rate of appearances towards the end of the exposition, at 22–9) is related to similar figures in the first movement. Here prominent turn shapes are found, for instance, in the second theme from bar 44 and in the following excursion from bar 68. Ultimately these turns derive from similar shapes in the theme, for example the f^2–e^2–d^2–e^2 of bars 5–6, but more generally from the manner in which the melodic line turns back in on itself. In fact the turn becomes one of the characteristic melodic features of the whole work. In addition to its many appearances in the first two movements, it is heard constantly in the trio of the third movement. The minuet features a turn in its theme (bars 3, 27, and 39) as well as a cognate form in its 'countersubject' – see the e^1–f^1–d^1–e^1 in the second violin at bars 2–3. In the finale there is the literal form first heard at bar 10 in the second violin as well as such written-out versions as bar 8 in the cello and bar 49^2 on both violins.

One aspect of a multi-movement work, often neglected, that can give much greater coherence to the connections between movements is temporal organization. According to David Epstein's 'temporal umbrella' theory, multi-movement works are conceived in one basic tempo of which each movement represents a subdivision.[11] The equation for the present work would thus be: ♩. of I = ♩ of II = ♩ of III = ♩ of IV. Therefore the final two movements share the same basic crotchet pulse; the finale, though, sounds much faster than the minuet, because the 'base rate' of its rhythmic values is the semiquaver, whereas the minuet scarcely moves beyond crotchets. This understanding of temporal relationships, which must of course be conceived as a broad principle rather than a precise requirement in performance, can make motivic interconnections more intelligible. For instance, given the ♩. = ♩ relationship of the first two movements the (elaborated) fall of a third at bar 8 of the Adagio should occupy much the same time-span as the fall from G to E in 10–11 of the Vivace. Another example: the opening unit of the minuet has much in common with the transitional shape in the Vivace at, for instance, bars 14–15. Haydn's bowing of the minuet unit is what makes the connection conceivable. The slur across the g^1–g^2 octave at the start demands a portamento or glissando treatment that approximates to the rising scale g^2 to g^3 of the first movement. The absence of bowing marks for the following three notes means a different bow-stroke for each note, again a similar type of articulation to the quaver-plus-rest forms of the Vivace. Given the proposed 3:2 proportions of crotchet pulse in the respective movements, the rising octave will cover nearly the same time-span in both its manifestations: one crotchet beat in the minuet and just over a beat and a half in the Vivace (from half-way through bar 14 to the downbeat of 15).

Another basic musical parameter that can very directly affect our perception of unity in a large-scale work, and one also usually neglected, is texture. The C major Quartet has a specific textural feature that can be thought of as thematic in its own right. This is the use of pairs of thirds in inner voices in the middle of the texture and in a middle register. They are, of course, found in the opening theme of the Vivace, in second violin and viola, moving from e^1 and g^1 up by a third and then back down again. They then occur in the transition to the second theme and in the second theme itself (35–42 then 43–50), as well as in the following harmonic excursion (see 70ff.). In the Adagio the most prominent example is the previously-discussed falling-third shape at bar 8. In the minuet they occur in the form of the thirds that constantly accompany the head-motive, as at 2–3 in second violin and cello.

It is in the finale, however, that Haydn takes most full account of this textural device: the movement actually opens with the 'accompanying' thirds unaccompanied, in second violin and viola. Here is the classical finale function of clarifying and regularizing. Indeed, as a gesture these thirds recall the opening theme of the Vivace; both inner-voice passages involve the use of repeated notes, staccato, with three initial pairs being heard. Typically, however, what was an implicitly regular pattern in the first movement, the total picture confused by the nature of the first violin line, is made more overtly symmetrical in the finale. From this point the thirds dominate much of the movement, now turning up at all levels of the texture.

Another vital feature running through the quartet involves the exploitation of the first strong dissonance we hear. In this work the note is C♯, as indeed it will be in the F major Quartet, No. 5. The recurrence of this note at so many important junctures and the influence it has on shaping the structure are not the result of a conscious intellectual decision by the composer; rather, Haydn's ear seems to be naturally drawn back to this discordant detail time and again. The C♯ is first heard on violin I at bar 3, where it is dissonant both horizontally, as a chromatic inflection of the rising line, and vertically – it is sounded against a C♮ in the cello. The restatement of the theme omits the cello's expected tonic notes at bars 21 and 23, so that when it does enter with a C♯ at bar 25, the dissonant character of the note is heightened. It also produces a dramatic diminished seventh chord which must resolve to II before the ensuing cadence (compare IV at the equivalent bar 7), a significant development in view of the minuet's later harmonic problems. At bars 34³–5 we hear parallel unisons on C♯–D between the two violins, lending a further edge to the dissonance. Charles Rosen has spoken in other contexts of Haydn's violation of part-writing etiquette in order to project an important disso-nance more forcefully.[12] Following this, at bars 35ff., there is a more subtle play on the C♯. The scales ascending from D in cello and first violin (deriving, of course, from the previously-discussed bars 14–15) seem undecided as to whether the penultimate note should be C♮ or C♯. Both are heard several times, creating a subtle blur for the listener at this quick speed; the standard editions give uniform C♯s throughout the passage. At bar 41 the cello reverts, seemingly decisively, to the C♯, before it is repeated then cancelled by a C♮ in the following bar.

The flat-side harmonic excursion from bar 65 results from the translation of the previous D♯ at 59 into an enharmonic E♭, but it seems Haydn is most interested in this remote harmonic area because it allows him also to reinterpret and dwell on the C♯ enharmonically. The first violin line from bar 68 emphasizes the D♭–C progression over and over, each time differently harmonized. Its larger shape is simply that of the inner parts' transition at bars 35–40, which in turn fused their repeated notes of the opening bars with the cadential close at bars 8–9. For all its apparently generous variety, the movement is as tightly controlled as any in Op. 50, and every shape is directly reused at least once – the enigmatic falling third of bars 10–11, for instance, is incorporated and normalized in the exposition's final cadential flourish (bars 101ff.). The D♭ in the present passage is finally resolved when it is replaced by a D♮ at 77², accompanied by the same chord in the same spacing as at bar 12. This is the turning-point from which a route can be found back to G major, although the second violin at bar 84 incorporates C♯ and C♮ in its transitional phrase, as the cello did at bar 42.

The clashing C♯ continues to register through the rest of the movement. It is naturally less emphatic in the resolving recapitulation, whose unusual literalness – for Haydn – inheres in the block-like syntax of the movement. The only exception to this literalness of return is the insertion of a block of fugato material recalling the procedures of the development. At the end of this section the C♯ subtly insinuates itself once more. At bars 218, 220, and 222 Haydn could just as easily have written C♮s as C♯s; the harmonic sense would be unaltered. However, his ear seems to have been drawn to the sharper note once again.

Haydn evidently found the theme of this movement a profitable one. He reshaped it in the first movement of Op. 74 No. 1 and then in the minuet of the same work, which also features a harmonic excursion through A♭ major. It evidently appealed to Beethoven as a fruitful model as well, for it emerges in the scherzo of his previously-mentioned Op. 18 No. 1 (compare also bars 11ff. of the Beethoven with bars 66ff. of the present movement).

The C♯ then plays a crucial part in the Adagio, first seen in the c^2–c♯^{2}–d^2 progression of bars 4–5. As in the first movement, C♯ initiates the move away from the tonic, even though the Adagio is in the subdominant key. At bar 17 in the second violin it prompts a move through D minor towards the dominant, C major. As well as more incidental appearances, for instance at bars 25, 29, and 51, it once more assumes a pivotal role in the coda. Here it is treated in both directions: c^1–c♯^{1}–d^1 at 54–5 in the cello, leading once more to D minor, followed by the enharmonic db^1–c^1 at bar 57. At the climax of the 'sentimental' flourish of bar 58 C♯ is once more highlighted for us: the rising chromatic scale stops when we reach this point and is followed by a leap to e^2, forming the most poignant part of the final cadential delay. C♯ is once again the first foreign note to be introduced in the minuet, but here it has momentous harmonic consequences. The proliferation of C♯s leads the movement into the D minor 'cul-de-sac' described earlier by David Wyn Jones. The harmonic problems faced by the minuet are thus a logical outcome of the insistence on the pivotal dissonant note through the course of the work. The trio features just the one appearance, but the cello's c♯ at bar 76, as mentioned before, plays an important role in the harmonic drama of the movement as a whole.[13]

The first violin's c♯^{2} at bar 29 of the finale once more initiates the harmonic movement away from the tonic, but the C♯ appropriately plays a less disruptive role in the concluding movement. Its appearances tend to be less structural in import than of an inflectional character, as at bars 60 and 175. Most notably it appears in the violin I line from bar 191 (transposed from 56ff.), which now constitutes a virtual quotation at pitch from the theme of the first movement (with the inner thirds below). Another near-quotation is provided by the cadential bars 221–3^1, which are uncannily similar to bars 282–4^1 of the first movement. In both passages the cello plays a repeated G, violin I and viola trill on d^2 and b^1 respectively, and violin II plays a thematically relevant part centering on f^1. Given the stereotyped character of most of the material here, one hardly hears this connection with the same vividness as the one previously described. Rather, the fourth-movement passage constitutes a 'rhyme' with the earlier one, testifying to the retentive aural memory of the composer for texture and sonority.

The finale also distinguishes itself by making a strong case for the observance of second-half repeat marks. The very ending of the movement is unusual in that it closes effectively with a solo phrase for the cello, particularly odd after the unanimity of the chord in the upper parts. In fact, if the repeat of the second part is taken, this makes an interesting 'transition' back to the start of the development. The second violin's d^1–e^1–f^1 at bars 229–30 is answered by the same figure in a unison D–E–F at 86–7. The cello's final shape is then 'answered' by all three other instruments in turn at bars 88–92 (viola then first then second violin) to the same accompanying chordal rhythm as at the end. One might therefore say that the need to repeat the second half is 'composed in', that the start of the development is written so as to be heard after the end of the recapitulation as well as the exposition – a fine joining together of two very large 'blocks' of music.

No. 3 in E♭ major

The third quartet is the most concise of the group. Initiated by a 'theme' of outrageous brevity, the work tends throughout towards contraction, neatness, and economy. Indeed, its obvious unity and self-sufficiency become almost oppressive; relief is provided by a quickish slow movement that does not reveal its structure and shape until it is almost over.

The economy can be found in all aspects of the work. Thematically, the connections are very clear; the outer movements and the trio all begin with an upbeat B♭ leading to an E♭, with a continuation by stepwise ascent through a prominent F. The minuet begins simply with an extended variant of this pattern, which procedurally almost suggests the 'chiming' openings of movements in many Baroque suites. Both outer movements also explicitly reuse their related opening themes as a 'second subject' to confirm the dominant. The meanness with material reaches its height in the last two movements. The minuet's opening rhythmic unit is heard in virtually every bar of the piece, while the finale not unexpectedly takes economy to the point of parody. The development starts identically to the beginning except for the cello's D♭; not only that, but the preceding phrase that closes the exposition at bars 65–74 is used verbatim to close the development and lead us back to yet another hearing of the opening theme. Thus the movement seems to be continually chasing its own tail.

Harmonically the pattern set up in the first two bars of the first movement proves influential. Root-position chords of tonic and dominant abound, especially in alternation as at the opening or the close (40–4) of the exposition. Once more the final two movements display this emphatic simplicity most clearly – compare the bass lines of the trio and the first twenty-four bars of the finale. The slow movement provides the exception sextuplet rhythms but also includes some literal returns to the theme (bars 110–14 on first violin and 118ff. in the cello). At bars 126ff. the horn-call material from 88–92 returns – 'as we were saying before we were interrupted'. It is grounded by a constant tonic pedal in the cello – a harmonic necessity after this 'bass-less' movement – and an extended fragment from the original theme is superimposed over it.

Looking at the movement as a whole, a structure of ternary with coda is rather problematical, since the coda takes up nearly half the movement. Even Reginald Barrett-Ayres's useful term 'split coda'[16] cannot overcome this difficulty, since what splits it is a complete variation: the movement still has something to say before the closure and final confirmation of the tonic. The movement can of course be understood somewhat loosely as just a set of variations, but the alternation of literal and varied forms of the theme introduces a rondo element into the form. This is also implied on a larger scale: the form could be represented as A B A C (interrupted) A C/Coda. Somewhere in between the three principles of ternary, variation, and rondo lies the structural truth of the movement. With its combination of intellectual fascination and an irresistible sense of temporal control, this is the equal of any movement in Op. 50.

No. 4 in F♯ minor

Like the E♭ major quartet, the present work is characterized by great tautness of construction, but to a very different end. It is difficult to imagine two works that contrast more strongly in mood: while No. 3 seems content in its world of an almost overplayed unity, No. 4 appears constricted and inhabits a world of what David Wyn Jones calls 'impersonal pathos'.[17] The opening Allegro spiritoso brings an unsettled quality that will remain for the whole work. Its use of the minor key is tense rather than impassioned; the ethos of the minor-key works of the so-called *Sturm und Drang* period has been left behind. The tenderness and expansiveness that Mozart often brings to his minor-key works are quite foreign to Haydn's procedures here; Haydn responds to the minor key in an extra-concise, very unsensual manner. In terms of self-expression he becomes withdrawn and inarticulate – the conversational spirit of all the other quartets in Op. 50 is absent.

This constricted expression can be seen most keenly in the first two movements of the work. Donald Tovey has written that the first movement

to this tendency, with what Cecil Gray calls its 'disembodied' sound. This is because of a comparative lack of bass-line. Only on a few occasions does the cello underpin the texture in a traditional and secure manner; the *opera buffa*-style alternations of I and V are completely absent here. This goes hand in hand with the radically different syntactical style of the movement, whose sense of onward flow is quite at odds with the small-scale reiterations of the other movements. This is achieved either despite or because of the extremely regular four-bar subphrases, which follow each other with a hypnotic regularity.

By being set in the dominant, the slow movement also counteracts another strong harmonic tendency of the rest of the work. This is an inclination to move flatwards, first seen in the viola's strong low D♭ at bar 9, whose local function is to counterbalance the effect of the A♮ in bar 8. Several other examples from the outer movements are interrelated in terms of their structural placement. The cello begins the development of the first movement by turning at bar 45 to an A♭ to cancel out the leading note of the preceding dominant chord; at the equivalent point of the finale (bar 75) it plays the previously-mentioned D♭. This directs the tonality towards the subdominant A♭ major, before moving one step further to the flat side with D♭ major. In neither case is a root-position triad achieved, however. This feature is saved for bars 89–92, which briefly affirm the relative minor of D♭, B♭ minor. The ensuing sequence at bars 93–102 is the most memorable part of the finale and, in its further flatward orientation, provides a climax to the predominant harmonic colour of the work. At the end of this passage there is a lengthy preparation for the entry of the theme in F minor at bar 110. Although brief, this aural highlight recalls the F minor entry of the theme in the first movement at bars 59–62. Further long-range consistency is provided by the fact that the second, contrasting half of the first-movement theme also appears prominently in the development in F minor, at bars 83–5.

The minuet moves even more strongly to the flat side by featuring a complete central section in G♭ major (from bar 17). Even the slow movement has a complete section in B♭ minor. This consistent use of flat-side colouring naturally lends the work a highly individual character. Flat-side keys such as the subdominant and the tonic minor tend to reinforce the tonic key; for this reason, they are often used in a recapitulation to counterbalance the typical sharp-side, dominant tendency of the preceding parts of the form. Thus their prominence here is part of the compactness of the whole work, part of its predilection towards reiteration and reinforcement. The work consequently has the lowest 'specific gravity' of any in Op. 50. It is also, one might say, the most consonant sounding quartet of its group.

The compactness of the quartet can also be seen in terms of other parameters. It uses a comparatively restricted pitch range and tends to hover around the middle registers; textures are also typically close and full. There is, for instance, no textural situation remotely like that heard at the end of the following work (see bars 73ff. of the finale of No. 4, where the instruments are paired and play in octaves far apart from each other), nor one akin to, say, the openness of the trio of No. 1. Articulation is also extremely consistent and becomes one of the most important structural features of the work. The governing pattern is slurred pairs interspersed with staccato notes, with repeated notes often also playing a part. This can be seen, for instance, in both theme and accompaniment of the finale; it forms the *raison d'être* of the minuet. It occurs in all sorts of contexts apart from the obvious main thematic ones: note, for example, its part in the subsidiary themes of the first movement at bars 25 and 34. It is almost equally prominent in the slow movement.

The other exceptional feature of the work is the playing with large-scale structure in the first two movements. As already mentioned, both of these contradict our formal expectations in their second halves. In the first movement, according to Charles Rosen, 'Haydn plays a wonderful historical joke by recalling an old-fashioned convention.' This convention, from the mid-eighteenth century, involves the appearance of the first phrase of the main theme in the dominant at the start of the second half, while the second is played in the tonic to mark the beginning of the recapitulation. Thus Haydn begins the reprise at bar 87^6 with the second half of the original theme. To add to the confusion, it is preceded by a false reprise of this material in the subdominant at 81^6–3^5. This is followed by a looser kind of false reprise in F minor, where the second half of the theme is harmonized and somewhat reshaped. There is in fact some justification in the preceding music for the false-sounding real reprise of the second part that follows: the first part has been heard in complete form, at pitch, in the viola at bars 63^6–6. In any case, Haydn quickly veers off course after this moment of recapitulation, and the rest of the section is condensed to a transposed form of bars 24–40^4.

Following bar 111, the apparent end of the movement, we have two bars of silence. Then the first half of the theme returns in the tonic, formally beginning the coda section. For Rosen this provides 'one of the rare

moments when a knowledge of history is necessary to enhance one pleasure in Haydn's wit'.[14] However, this feature does not just represen playing with convention of a sort that occurs throughout Op. 50. The sp reprise is also a product of the disunity of the theme. Just as the origin antecedent and consequent are improbably far apart stylistically, so Hay gives each half its own recapitulation, well separated in temporal term The coda then attempts to mediate between and overcome the stylis disunity of the two halves. Haydn provides a transition between the two bars 117–21 so that the second half is now prepared harmonically thematically. He gradually alters the last unit of the first part, at 116^6– so that the first violin's shape at 120^6–1 can, upon repetition, lead natur into the rustic strain. This is now accompanied by a bass-line rhythm matches that in the first part of the theme and by an inner-voice shape anticipates bars 13ff. of the finale. The unison treatment then retu extended through four bars to lead naturally to the final peroration.

The slow movement presents a more radical type of disruption. We only grasp its form at all when it is almost over. Haydn must have enjo keeping himself and his players guessing, for he repeated the idea alr immediately in the finale of the Quartet, Op. 54 No. 2; this plays on convention of the slow introduction, but turns out eventually to b Adagio finale![15] The present movement allows one to change one's st tural opinions several times. When the theme returns at bars 48^4–56 preceding tonic minor section is cast in the light of a trio, a *minore* b primarily on the first four notes of the theme. It could also be unders as a variation, but few if any variation sets of the time follow their th immediately by a variation in the opposite mode. Thus a straightfor ternary structure seems most likely at this point. From 56^4 onw however, the theme is varied, especially by the use of chromatic inflec which undoubtedly reflect the influence of the 'trio'. Then bars 7 present a literal return of the third period of the theme (16–24).

There then follows a repeated eight-bar section which could be an freer variation on the theme than the preceding *minore*. It might at firs be heard as the start of a coda, but by bar 88 (unlike the theme) moved firmly to the dominant. Its continuation expands the hor motive of bars 82^4–4^3, with rising sextuplets answering the cello's sh 88. After two bars the motive passes to the lower pair of instrume reference to the textural pairing in the presentation of the original t Just when we expect a return to bars 81ff., however, a complete varia the theme is inserted (from 94^4). This is mostly expressed in th

shows for the first time Haydn's definite renunciation of tragic ends to sonata movements, and his now typical association of the minor mode with a passionate, somewhat blustering temper, ending with a recapitulation (in these circumstances regular) in the tonic major, so that everything turns out well. As he said of himself, 'Anybody can see that I'm a good-natured fellow.'

He then gives the conclusion of this first movement the status of a 'happy end'. These judgments rather ignore the sense in which the major-key ending of the Allegro spiritoso has more to do with the major-minor balance of the whole work than with Haydn's desire for a 'happy end'. A minor ending here would be too sour and fraught in the larger context. As it stands, the conclusion represents a moment of 'false dawn', a necessary reinforcement of the structural relaxation of the reprise by a *tierce de Picardie*. Since the finale ends in the minor key, it is incumbent upon the first movement not to overburden the work as a whole.

In any case, the major ending is hardly emphatic or expansive. The recapitulation is almost perfunctorily regular once the major is reached at bar 148; there are no elaborations or insertions and there is no coda. The movement may be said to be 'cut off' rather than resolved. This lack of real finality throws the weight of expectation onto events yet to come. It is as if the first part of the story ends with an uneasy truce; a genuine 'happy end' would require some recomposition that acknowledged the strife of what had gone before and therefore resolved the issue more fully.

Of the second movement Tovey says:

It is a pity that [Haydn] did not see fit to provide the variations of his andante with a few bars of coda; the contrast between the two themes is grand, but the impression left by the unexpanded end of the whole is perfunctory.[18]

Once more he rather misses the point. The Andante is cut off just like the first movement; the abruptness of its conclusion is emphasized by the weird scoring of the final chord and its staccato articulation. This provides a rather brutal final word for the sweetness of the major-key sections, and the astringency of the minor-key sections is momentarily revived. The slow movement of course continues the major-minor battle of the first movement, which is now built into the structure by the use of double-variation form. It too, as we have just seen, ends rather underwhelmingly in the major.

The third movement also builds the major-minor tension into its structure, the major-key minuet surrounding the developmental minor-key trio. As in the Andante and to some extent in the first movement, mode is consistently allied to texture. Thus all the major-key sections are predominantly homophonic in expression while minor-key sections tend to be contrapuntal. The *minore* of the Andante, for instance, is more a texture than a second theme as such. Keller cites it as stressing 'the contrapuntal end of our nameless, intrinsic quartet texture';[19] thus while the texture is clearly not polyphonic in any precise sense, neither can any of its parts be described as truly subordinate or accompanimental. Indeed, the theme presents a tortured kind of dialogue in a very full texture; this quality is most evident in the dragging imitation between first violin and cello at bars 28^4–32. The textural contrast is just as marked in the third movement, especially since the minuet features so much unison writing; this refers to the texture that opened the work and helps to prepare for the extraordinary bars 62–4 of the finale.

Given the structural association of mode with texture, when Haydn chooses to write a minor-key finale it is quite logical that it too should be polyphonic – in fact, a fugue. This is the largest-scale way in which the fugal finale is 'prepared' by the preceding movements. Indeed, there is some sense of inevitability about the movement: it strategically gathers up various motivic and textural threads from the first three movements in a manner that was rather less apparent in Op. 20. There the fugal finales formed a climax to the musical argument but in a less closely controlled context.

Another textural preparation is provided by the theme of the first movement. This is a model for the unsettled procedures that follow, reflected for instance in the equivocation of the inner parts at bars 21–4 of the Allegro spiritoso or the textural extreme of bars 38–42.[20] The tutti presentation of the motto of the movement is succeeded by a solo for first violin, *piano*, which introduces the sighing appoggiaturas so prevalent in the whole work. Its following phrase at 4^2–8^1 ends on the tonic, but the sense of perfect cadence there is relatively weak. Because of the phrase structure, the ear tends rather to hear the diminished seventh of 6^1 leading to the tonic chord at 8^1. The whole phrase is then imitated by the viola and then by the cello, each time reharmonized so as to finish in the mediant, A major. This extension means, as Günter Thomas notes, that the theme's 'formal boundaries are unclear'.[21] The whole passage also provides a kind of horizontal polyphony, with its sense of repeated subject entry, that anticipates the process of the finale. Later in the movement, the motto theme itself is treated contrapuntally (bars 100–12).

The shape of the fourth movement's fugue theme is also inherent in material we have already heard (see Example 13). Its falling sixth recalls the same interval in the motto of the first movement (for instance F♯ to A at bars 1–2), which was heard at each new juncture of the form. The slightly larger shape in the fugue theme, the first three notes D–C♯–E♯, is quite directly anticipated by the Andante's opening *minore* unit (see the G♯–A–C of the cello. The sixth C–A is also present in compound, vertical form on the downbeat of bar 21, with C in the cello and A in the viola. This produces an extraordinary sound, quite untranslatable in keyboard, or indeed orchestral, terms). The turns of the second part of the fugue theme follow a pattern of turn on a weak beat leading to a strong-beat rise in pitch. This has been heard in the opening bars of both Andante and minuet, although the most exact precedent is provided by the tonic-minor trio. The viola subject begins with a turn on the same pitches as bar 2 of the finale (G♯–F♯–E♯–F♯); its following rising seventh (later heard also as a rising fifth and octave) opens a wide gap in the melodic line that has a similar effect to the falling sixth of the fugue theme. Both leaps are then partially filled in by stepwise movement in the opposite direction. The second violin's countersubject in the trio seems to rearrange the turn pattern of the finale (E♯–G♯–F♯ at bars 1–2: compare F♯–E♯–G♯ at the start of the

Example 13 Op. 50 No. 4

Example 14 Op. 50 No. 4

trio). Both shapes are of course just simplified versions of the predominant full-turn figure.

The most characteristic sound of the work, and one to which the finale again gives more urgent and coherent expression, is the diminished seventh. It occurs at every possible opportunity in the minor-key sections, but it also insinuates itself into the major-key parts of the work. The diminished seventh is implied for instance at bars 6 and 29 of the minuet. It also provides many harmonic twists in the A major theme of the Andante, the most notable being the appearances at bars 5^2 and 18^1. These stand out because of the unexpected colour they give to the reappearances of the opening melodic unit. The trio also features a *fz* shudder to the ubiquitous chord at bar 66.

The climax to the use of the diminished seventh arrives in two 'waves'.[22] The first, from bar 62 of the finale, leads to a hectic recollection of the first movement's 'second subject' (from I/bars 28ff.). The texture is virtually identical, with semiquaver figuration on alternating notes in the inner parts, tonic-dominant crotchet pairs in the cello, and a melodic line that emphasizes a cell of three repeated notes (see Example 14).

At bar 70 comes the first of the two *ff* markings, the only such indications in Op. 50 (see Illustration 2). The following passage opens up a very wide registral gap between the two pairs of instruments, an extraordinary sound which then explodes into the ultimate expression of the diminished seventh. Bars 77 to 82 stride up and down the same diminished seventh chord on B♯ in truly grisly fashion, filling in the preceding registral space, before a quiet resolution to the dominant chord at bar 83. The strained sonority that has dominated much of the quartet is transformed into a sound whose sense of discomfort is vivid.

It is this feeling of strain that has been underappreciated by commentators on the work. Rosemary Hughes calls the closing fugue 'uncompromisingly tragic',[23] Tovey 'the quietest and deepest of all instrumental fugues since Bach, [striking] a note so tragic that Beethoven's C sharp minor quartet is the first thing one can connect with it'.[24] Rosen comments that 'the element of academic display present in almost all classical fugues loses itself completely in pathos'.[25] Talk of 'tragedy', however, implies a grandeur and nobility that the quartet does not possess, while 'pathos' implies a certain tenderness that is also foreign to the aesthetic of the work. It is too bitter in sound and mood to be 'pathetic'; in fact, the mood of the work never really declares itself. By constantly constricting the flow of the music, with the exception of the finale's bars 77–82, full self-expression is never attained. The profound agitation of the work finds no satisfying outlet.

No. 5 in F major

The F major Quartet shows perhaps more textural self-awareness than any other work of Op. 50. The exceptional slow movement, the monothematic minuet and trio and the finale with its portamento theme all show an interest in textural manipulation that is initiated by the opening theme of the first movement. Keller describes the opening period as a 'subtle climax of quartet textures'.[26] Beginning with a duet for the two violins, the entry of the viola and cello on an octave C♯ provides a disruption of great structural importance. C♯ will play a crucial role in the whole work, just as it did in No. 2. For instance, when the opening unit is repeated again from bar 24 the C♯ is superimposed upon it to begin the transition to the dominant.[27] The larger problem of the opening theme is the lack of bass support prior to the C♯. This is apparently solved when in the recapitulation Haydn adds an octave F then C in the lower instruments at bars 103 and 105.

However, in the coda that follows another highly abbreviated recapitulation Haydn once more capitalizes on the shock provided by bar 5. The coda begins at bar 133, with the opening unit now being combined with the pitches of the closing unit of bars 7–8. This is followed by three playings of the second two-bar thematic unit, increasing the sense of anticipation. There has been no bass-line support for this version of the theme. A two-bar silence follows before the consequent phrase is heard again at 143–7. In other words, having 'normalized' or 'explained' the opening at the start of the reprise, Haydn decides he wants to have his fun over again. Then, finally, the violins' ♪ | ♩ figures, having always previously been invariant in pitch, yield to the rising-semitone urge of the indecorous lower parts. Starting on C and proceeding upwards via D♭ (C♯ enharmonically), it is the upper duo which now leads, the lower parts following contentedly in their wake. There is a conversational logic to this textural reversal – having finally won the argument, having persuaded the upper pair to see matters their way, viola and cello are quite happy to be 'supportive'. They no longer withhold their bass-line services and imitate the violins bar for bar until the dominant finally arrives in bar 156. From bar 158 another sort of textural resolution occurs; for the first and only time in the movement, the antecedent phrase is played by all four instruments. This 'tutti' finally brings together the textural pairings that have dominated much of the movement.

The structural role that texture assumes in this movement brings us to another paradox in the Haydn string quartet: for all the conversational spirit apparent in Op. 50 and other sets, Haydn is far less punctilious in the distribution of melodic material than, for instance, Mozart is in his 'Haydn' quartets. If the melodic leadership is more equally distributed in Mozart's quartets, then it ought to follow that his works in the genre demonstrate a more genuine sense of conversation, yet the opposite is the case. The allocation of melodic material in Mozart often suggests a process of quasi-formal exchange, in which the meaning of the line transferred from one instrument to another remains roughly the same. This is the conversational equivalent of nodding approval. In the Haydn quartet, on the other hand, the sense of role-playing is more subtly conceived; as we have just seen in the first movement of No. 5, the viola and cello are able in a sense to dominate the texture, even though they play almost no melodic material. They seem to be applying the Pinteresque principle, as it were, that victory in the conversational arena is achieved not so much by what is said as by what is (deliberately) not said. By withholding the expected response at the start of the movement, they can dictate the course of the action.

In a broader sense, the unpredictable rate of exchange of material and sharper definition of roles (as opposed to Mozart's more symmetrically conceived turn-taking) allows the Haydn string quartet a full repertoire of conversational devices – agreements, disagreements, longueurs, overtalking, interruptions, and all manner of gradations between a collective and an individual inflection of subject-matter. This provides a somewhat different interpretation of string-quartet texture to the absolute equality of the four parts deemed by so many writers to be the ideal for the form. Indeed, even in the Mozart quartets the first violin remains clearly the 'leader', assuming responsibility for most of the melodic presentation. This is simply a corollary of the natural tendency of the ear to gravitate towards the top of a musical texture. Mozart and Haydn found different strategies for undermining or deflecting this natural first-violin dominance, with Mozart's solutions tending to the formal while Haydn's were rather more intimate and versatile.

Part of the charm of the first movement of No. 5 lies, as mentioned earlier, in its slightly old-fashioned metrical sense; this gives some of the material the quality of a divertimento. With its sextuplets, solid quaver pulse and Allegro moderato marking, this is distinctly less up-to-date than the first movements of Nos. 1 and 6. Confirmation of an older pedigree

Example 15 'Op. 3 No. 5', movement IV

may be obtained by comparing it with the 2/4 Scherzando movement of the Quartet 'Op. 3 No. 5', not by Haydn (see Example 15).

A further trait of the older style is the sudden breaking into sextuplets at bars 20, 36, and 54 of the exposition. The recent rediscovery of the autograph of the quartet has shown that bars 20–3 were inserted as an afterthought. The music originally proceeded directly from bar 19 to bar 24.[28] Haydn no doubt added bars 20–3 precisely so as to prepare for the later outbursts of animation. The rhythmic structure of the exposition is consequently better balanced; the dominant account of the theme is now preceded, split, and followed by the skittish sextuplet rhythms. This split account, antecedent phrase commencing at bar 24 (initially in the tonic), consequent at 46, presages the events of the coda.

The slow movement does not refer significantly to the C♯. The most important feature it shares with the first movement is a heightened textural awareness. An instance of this is the principle of contrary-motion scalic lines that occurs in several different contexts, from bars 5–6 to 15–16 (one line against three) to the pairs of contrary-motion thirds at bars 19–20. This latter sonority in fact has an equivalent in the first movement: see bars 98–101 and especially the 'tutti' at 158–62. Melodically the Poco adagio also takes up a number of first-movement hints. The very opening note, f^2 in the first violin, represents a kind of resolution denied to the first movement; in the final flourish there the first violin lands on the mediant a^2 in the final bar when we might have expected to hear the more conclusive-sounding tonic note. The melodic shape that begins with this note, f^2 to bb^2 at bars 1–3 of the second movement, recalls the first violin's c^2 to f^2 of I/134–5, which also occurred in conjunction with inner-voice thirds. Indeed, the leader's entire melodic line from bars 134–7 of the first movement seems to anticipate features of the slow movement (see Example 16). Its larger initial shape, the ascending octave c^2 to c^3 with a longer first note, is heard at $5–6^1$ of the Poco adagio. The dotted-rhythmic form in which it is expressed here suggests a fusion of the first-movement scale with the dotted rhythms that follow at bars 136–7. This rhythmic shape is especially striking in the context of the first movement, since it is heard nowhere else there; this reinforces its preparatory role.

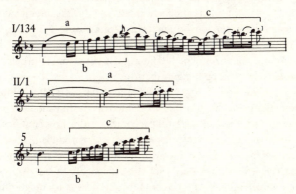

Example 16 Op. 50 No. 5

The cadential tag that ends the consequent phrase in the Poco adagio at $7^2–8^1$, found at a number of strategic points later in the movement, is indebted to the identical feature in bars 19 and 53 of the first movement.

After its use there the figure is neglected until it is more consistently employed in the slow movement.

The minuet and trio share the propensity of Op. 50's other third movements for playing games with harmonic movement and proportions. The particular fetish for dominant preparation is once again evident in the current minuet. Here it seems to last for too long, beginning at bar 16 and continuing past the point of melodic reprise at bar 23. Indeed the first strong root-position tonic chord of the movement is heard only in bar 33, in conjunction with a now familiar cadential tag in the violins. The comparative weakness of the tonic chord is also apparent in the first period. At bar 5 it seems to be a passing thought after the four-bar emphasis on the dominant seventh, and the profusion of B♮s indicates that the composer's thoughts are already heading towards the establishment of C major. In order to right the balance, Haydn needs a double reprise (a procedural echo of the first movement). The first, at bar 23, stings us with a C♯ replacing the expected C♮ above the over-extended dominant pedal. It then expands the original consequent phrase with a significant hint of the subdominant in the cello's E♭ at 29; this is needed to compensate for the overweening role of the dominant thus far. In the subsequent cadence at bars 31–3 root-position tonic and dominant chords are heard in conjunction for the first time. The second reprise, from bar 33, is, like that of the first movement, really a coda. It begins by cancelling the previous C♯, but the second violin joins in in canon a beat later, so that the attempt at reprise turns into an extension of the antecedent phrase. As if in desperation, Haydn turns to a rhythmic device to emphasize the plain F–B♭–C–F bass-line of the final bars. The hemiolas raise the temperature in preparation for the vehement opening of the trio.

Because of the double, but unsatisfactory, reprise of the minuet, the monothematicism of the trio has an immediate justification. It provides compensation for the lack of a proper return within the confines of the minuet. First of all the antecedent phrase is reproduced, although in unison rather than as a solo and with more aggressive articulation. The repetition veers off course only with the unison D♭ of bar 44, the most dramatic interpretation of the C♯ in the work. The consequent phrase of the minuet theme is then reintroduced and reworked after the double bar (note the E♭–A♭–E♭–B♭ outline of the first violin at 55–8). The trio also continues the idea of the double reprise. First of all there is a textural recapitulation from bar 63, but not a harmonic or a precise thematic one. After a cadence at 72^2–5^1 that is very close in contour to the one at bars

30^2–3^1 of the minuet, the thematic reprise arrives in the cello (but with Db replacing D♮). It comes so late, however, as to constitute more of a coda.

The 'chord-pendulum' of the final Vivace acts as the textural simplifying agent that is required after the complications of the three previous movements. The finale is full of echoes of these movements, on all levels. For instance, the closing cadential figure at bars 7–8 of the first movement theme is replicated at the same structural point in the finale, bars 11–12. The C♯ makes a pivotal appearance at the beginning of the development section (bar 55), although it makes an impact earlier on as a low Db (cello, bars 5–6). The extension by canon of the minuet antecedent at bars 33–7 is reworked in the finale at bars 41–3. The G pedal beneath combined with the G♯ in viola and first violin at 41^6 also reminds us of the situation at the minuet's first reprise, in bars 23–4. In fact the contour of the minuet's antecedent phrase is also suggested by the first violin at bars 30–1 of the finale. When Haydn reaches the equivalent point in his recapitulation (bars 104–5), he recomposes the ending of the phrase so as to get in another C♯–D progression.

The finale of No. 5 was the last movement of the opus to be finished, to Haydn's evident relief. A lack of time can produce great music, but in truth this is the one disappointing movement of Op. 50. There is no evident weakness to which one can point, but somehow the movement is too straightforward structurally. The resolving character of the finale appears to be taken too far, with the result that the movement has insufficient internal tension. One might expect, for instance, some manipulation of its most characteristic sound, the single-string portamento first heard at bars 3–4, but, unlike the virtuosic treatment of the *bariolage* in the finale in No. 6, it remains unvaried. The second half of the movement passes by too fluently with a complete absence of surprises, and it is perhaps primarily for this reason that the finale fails to convince.

No. 6 in D major

The final quartet of Op. 50 is the grandest and richest of the set. Its characteristic sound inheres partly in the open-string key of D major. It is the most consistently loud work of the opus, highly chromatic in its tonal language and full of dense, complicated textures. The work is also characterized by a drive towards cadence points that take a long time to arrive. Rosen, cited earlier, notes that in the first movement 'there is no cadence on the dominant until almost the end of the exposition'.[29] Haydn postpones it for as long as possible by means of a lengthy excursion in F major (bars 38ff.); it finally arrives at 47–8. The only other perfect cadence in the exposition – apart from the one that opens the work and necessitates all the later cadential deflections – is in the tonic at bars 15–16. Its effect is undermined, however, by the fz at 15^2, which deaccentuates the expected strong downbeat at 16^1. When we arrive at this beat, the cello then further diffuses the cadence; its fz D acts not so much as the root of a D major tonic chord as the beginning of a new thematic unit.

It has already been suggested that the first movement as a whole lacks a firm sense of closure. It finishes quietly and unemphatically, the aural picture complicated by a number of chromatic inflections. The violin's bb^1 at 161–2 remains explicitly unresolved in terms of register. As with the first two movements of No. 5, but more sharply felt here, the expected resolution occurs at the beginning of the slow movement. The first violin arches up from the d^1 that ended the first movement to the resolving a^1 on the first downbeat of the Poco adagio. The slow movement itself, however, does not tarry at its end. It, too, finishes in low-key manner with an exact transposition into D major of the closing four bars of its exposition. This is particularly noticeable given the grandeur of its larger design. Significantly, this is the only slow movement of Op. 50 to be cast in unabridged sonata form, with a full – and eventful – development section. The minuet, too, ends without a flourish; the opening eight-bar theme is simply repeated, constituting something of a throw-away ending. The trio falls into line by determinedly and chromatically procrastinating over its final cadence (see bars 78–83), so that once more a major point of structural articulation is de-emphasized. The *Sieg[ue]* indications that literally link the last three movements of the work are, it has been pointed out, simply a logical consequence of this restless forward drive.

The closing phrase that opens the work may be seen in its more normal and typical context in the first movement of the G major Quartet, Op. 77 No. 1, at bars 12–14 (see Example 17). Haydn clearly grew fond of the device. The slow introduction of Symphony No. 97 (1792) begins with another type of closing gesture, one which is reheard in a syntactically proper context first to close the introduction at bars 12–13 and then towards the end of the exposition in the Vivace (97–103). Sheltering under Epstein's 'temporal umbrella', it is rewritten in note values that will sound at roughly the same speed as its appearance in the slow introduction. A closing gesture also opens the finale of the D major Quartet, Op. 76 No. 5, but here the gesture does not consist of a melodic tag but a series of typically

Example 17 Op. 77 No. 1, movement I

emphatic closing chords. In this instance the pun is more structurally appropriate, since a finale as a whole obviously constitutes a finish; needless to say, the movement ends with the same chords. However, one does not have to look any further than Op. 50 itself to find comparable examples of a closing phrase. No. 1 of course starts with another type of closure, but what has been overlooked is that its final extended form in the coda includes, at bars 157–9, a falling shape that is very similar to bars 2–4 of the No. 6 theme (see Example 18).[30] The first part of the gesture is found in a 'proper' context even within the same work, in the first violin's descent from A to C♯ at bars 42–3 of the Poco adagio, closing the development section.

There is a more extraordinary echo of the Allegro's opening phrase elsewhere in the work. Amidst all the critical enthusiasm for the juggling of

Example 18 Op. 50 No. 1
Op. 50 No. 6

the *bariolage* technique in the finale, space has generally been found to note that the contrasting second subject at bars 48–56 derives from the fall of a fifth undergone by the principal theme of the movement from A to D. The weakness of this connection is that it does not account for the E♯ that follows the C♯ to F♯ descent at bar 50. Much more significant is the relationship of this phrase to the first six notes of the Allegro, with its longer first note and falling sixth expressed through semiquaver note values. The finale typically regularizes matters by repeating the falling-sixth unit twice more. Its continuation at 54–6 is then a near-match for bars 2–4 of the Allegro theme. Thus the whole phrase, with its *buffa*-style accompaniment, emerges as a parody of the first movement's opening/closing phrase.

The harmonic setting of the second subject is also significant. In F♯ minor, it relates by a third to the dominant A reached at bar 48. Median relationships are one of the most striking features of the entire work. In our immediate fourth-movement context, for instance, the dominant A of the exposition is also 'shadowed' at bars 64–7 by C major, a minor-third relationship that balances the preceding F♯ minor. However, this 'C major' is never explicitly stated; the recent rediscovery of the autographs has revealed that the e¹ found in the viola part at bar 67 of the traditional editions is inauthentic. In its place should stand an f♮¹ tied over from the preceding three bars. If this makes for a rather startling chord-progression from bar 67 to bar 68, the resulting sonority is entirely consistent with the complexity and 'bite' of the work's harmonic language. Among larger-scale examples the F major excursion of the first movement also stands a third away from the controlling dominant in that point of the exposition; likewise its B♭ major equivalent to D major in the recapitulation. In the slow movement the repeated dominant A of bar 10 leads without a formal modulation to F major in the following bar; then the F major at the end of the exposition is dramatically succeeded by D♭ major after the double bar, and A♭ major in bars 32–5 moves enharmonically to E. Across the double bar in the minuet D moves to F♯, anticipating the relationship in the finale more directly.

Even the *bariolage* of the finale's main theme provides a kind of parody. The repeated As that begin slow movement, minuet, and trio have become so insistent that the finale can only go one better by changing the colour within the repetitions. This cross-string sonority is, nevertheless, strongly prepared by the *forte* accompanimental oscillations of the Poco adagio, such as those heard in the inner parts at bars 26–31 and 37ff. The intervening passage at bars 32–6, which provides a moment of dramatic suspense in the middle of a busy work, also capitalizes on the repeated-note motive. In addition, it provides a fine example of the deployment of a comic-operatic technique (here involving the textural and harmonic handling of re-iteration) in a completely non-comic context.

However, the ultimate element of parody constitutes a virtual inter-movement quotation – at bars 229–31 of the last movement the first violin plays an isolated falling sixth from B to D, with a *fz* emphasizing the long initial note. This transposition of the opening phrase of the first movement resolves its dominant orientation by placing it in a secure D major context. The ensuing final bars provide another apparently understated ending, yet they also form a climax to the predominant sound of the movement. In the final phrase the upper three instruments all play a *bariolage* version of the notes of the tonic triad, while the cello approximates to their effect on its lowest string. 'These two cadential phrases', says Hans Keller, 'produce an unprecedented sound ... whose wit ... is in fact deeply moving'[31] – an appropriately double-edged ending to the opus.

Viewing Op. 50 as a whole, one could be wise after the event and say that the composer could not have gone on thus. In the Op. 54 quartets of 1788 Haydn turns to much broader and more obviously dramatic means of expression, as if to escape the severity of the task he had set himself in Op.

50. Yet, in spite of the consistent purity of the writing, the set contains enormous variety of character between and within individual works, as if the more logically and strictly Haydn defined his compositional starting points (specifically, his compositional 'problems'), the more freedom he would have in assessing the possible routes of continuation. Stravinsky proclaimed much the same principle nearly two hundred years later:

my freedom will be so much the greater and more meaningful the more narrowly I limit my field of action and the more I surround myself with obstacles ... The more constraints one imposes, the more one frees oneself of the chains that shackle the spirit.[32]

By the time of the composition of Op. 50, Haydn not only had achieved a measure of control over his creative life, he had achieved a magisterial control over its creative products.

Notes

Preface

1 'Did Haydn "synthesize" the Classical string quartet?', in *Haydn Studies: Proceedings of the International Haydn Conference, Washington, D.C., 1975*, ed. Jens Peter Larsen, Howard Serwer, and James Webster (New York-London: Norton, 1981), p. 336.

1 Origins of the genre

1 See Mary Sue Morrow, *Concert Life in Haydn's Vienna: Aspects of a Developing Musical and Social Institution* (New York: Pendragon Press, 1989), p. 161.
2 By Michael Tilmouth, for instance, in the entry 'String Quartet', *The New Grove Dictionary of Music and Musicians*, ed. Stanley Sadie (London: Macmillan, 1980), vol. 18, p. 277.
3 Quoted in H. C. Robbins Landon, *Haydn: Chronicle and Works*, 5 vols. (London: Thames and Hudson, 1976–80), vol. 1: *Haydn: The Early Years 1732–1765*, p. 64.
4 *Classic Music: Expression, Form and Style* (New York: Schirmer, 1980), p. 126.
5 Quoted in Landon, *Chronicle and Works*, vol. 1, p. 228.
6 See Rudolf Pečman, 'Alessandro Scarlatti: A predecessor of Joseph Haydn in the genre of the string quartet', in *Haydn Studies*, p. 459.
7 Pečman's term, ibid., p. 456.
8 *Chronicle and Works*, vol. 1, p. 254.

2 Development of the genre

1 'Franz Joseph Haydn', in *Cyclopedic Survey of Chamber Music*, comp. and ed. Walter Willson Cobbett (London: Oxford University Press, 1929), vol. 1, p. 539.
2 (Philadelphia: Lippincott, 1959), pp. 64–5.
3 Only part of the first movement is contained in the autograph fragment of 1771, but, given the character of the work, it is reasonable to assume that the rest was written fairly promptly.
4 *The String Quartet* (London: Thames and Hudson, 1983), p. 29.
5 H. C. Robbins Landon and David Wyn Jones, *Haydn: His Life and Music* (London: Thames and Hudson, 1988), pp. 163–4.
6 *The Great Haydn Quartets: Their Interpretation* (London: Dent, 1986), p. 51.
7 *The Collected Correspondence and London Notebooks of Joseph Haydn*, ed. H. C. Robbins Landon (London: Barrie and Rockliff, 1959), pp. 32–3.
8 *Classical Music: A Concise History from Gluck to Beethoven* (London: Thames and Hudson, 1986), p. 108.
9 *The Classical Style* (London: Faber and Faber, 1971), p. 118.
10 'Joseph Haydns künstlerische Persönlichkeit in seinen Streichquartetten', in *Syntagma Musicologicum: Gesammelte Reden und Schriften*, ed. Martin Ruhnke (Kassel: Bärenreiter, 1963), pp. 541–7.

11 *Haydn and the Enlightenment: The Late Symphonies and their Audience* (Oxford: Clarendon Press, 1990), p. 54.
12 Ibid., p. 74.
13 *The Classical Style*, p. 142.
14 *Haydn and the Enlightenment*, p. 62.
15 Ibid., pp. 57–8.
16 See the Preface, p. 7.

3 Capellmeister at Esterháza

1 Quoted in *Chronicle and Works*, vol. 2: *Haydn at Esterháza 1766–1790*, p. 42.
2 Quoted in *Chronicle and Works*, vol. 3: *Haydn in England 1791–1795*, pp. 189–91.
3 Ibid., p. 191.
4 *The Collected Correspondence*, pp. 24–5.
5 Ibid., p. 31.
6 See *Chronicle and Works*, vol. 2, pp. 668 ff.

4 Genesis

1 James Webster's phrase, quoted in *Chronicle and Works*, vol. 2, p. 578.
2 Ibid., p. 456.
3 'Haydn, Franz Joseph', *The New Grove*, vol. 8, p. 356.
4 *The Collected Correspondence*, p. 45.
5 Quoted in Robert Layton, *Sibelius* (The Master Musicians) (London: Dent, 1965), p. 40.
6 *The Collected Correspondence*, p. 45.
7 Günter Thomas, 'Haydn's "Prussian" Quartets', notes to recording by the Tokyo String Quartet (DGG 423 509–2; 1976), trans. John Coombs, p. 11. The translation in *The Collected Correspondence* reads: 'As to the Quartets, the agreement remains' (p. 46).
8 See *Chronicle and Works*, vol. 2, pp. 378–9.
9 All of the following excerpts from Haydn's letters may be found in *The Collected Correspondence*, pp. 56–69.
10 László Somfai, ['Six string quartets, Op. 50'], notes to recording by the Tátrai Quartet (HCD 11934–35–2; 1987), trans. Mária Steiner, p. 4.
11 *The Collected Correspondence*, pp. 70–6.
12 In his article 'Multistage variance: Haydn's legacy to Beethoven' (*The Journal of Musicology* 1/3 (1982), p. 273) Jan LaRue mentions his '[l]ong experience in discovering that Haydn has done everything first', ahead of his one-time pupil.
13 *The Collected Correspondence*, p. 34.
14 Ibid., p. 76.

5 The story of the autographs

1 I am indebted for much of the information in this account to Georg Feder, Christopher Hogwood, and the present owners of the autographs.
2 *Chronicle and Works*, vol. 2, p. 625.
3 'Joseph Haydn 1982: Gedanken über Tradition und historische Kritik', in *Proceedings of the International Joseph Haydn Congress, Wien, Hofburg, 5–12 September 1982*, ed. Eva Badura-Skoda (Munich: Henle, 1986), p. 604. My translation.
4 'Zur Textkritik von Haydns Streichquartetten', in *Festschrift Arno Forchert zum 60. Geburtstag am 29. Dezember 1985*, ed. Gerhard Allroggen and Detlef Altenburg (Kassel: Bärenreiter, 1986), p. 138. My translation.

6 Critical reception

1 *Foundations of Music History*, trans. J. B. Robinson (Cambridge: Cambridge University Press, 1983), p. 23.
2 'Haydn, Franz Joseph', *The New Grove*, vol. 8, p. 355.
3 *Haydn String Quartets* (BBC Music Guides) (London: BBC Publications, 1966), p. 33.
4 *The String Quartet*, p. 51.
5 *Haydn: A Creative Life in Music*, 2nd edn, revised and enlarged in collaboration with Irene Geiringer (London: G. Allen and Unwin, 1964), pp. 311–12.
6 *The String Quartet*, p. 52.
7 *The Classical Style*, pp. 138–9.
8 'The Significance of Haydn's Op. 33', in *Haydn Studies*, p. 445.
9 Ibid., p. 450.
10 ('Six string quartets, Op. 50'), p. 5.
11 See *The Classical Style*, pp. 138–9.
12 Ibid., pp. 128–9.
13 ('Six string quartets, Op. 50'), p. 6.
14 'Franz Joseph Haydn', *Cyclopedic Survey of Chamber Music*, p. 541.
15 *Haydn: His Life and Music*, p. 198.

7 Design

1 The finale of Op. 33 No. 1 is in sonata form.
2 *The Great Haydn Quartets*, p. 133.
3 ('Six string quartets, Op. 50'), p. 9.
4 *The Great Haydn Quartets*, p. 237. See also pp. 24–5.
5 *Haydn: His Life and Music*, pp. 199–200.
6 *The Classical Style*, p. 139.
7 See *The Great Haydn Quartets*, p. 88.
8 *Haydn: His Life and Music*, p. 199.
9 ('Six string quartets, Op. 50'), p. 8.
10 'Haydn's "Prussian" Quartets', p. 14.
11 For a discussion of tone in its Classical sense, see Rosen, *The Classical Style*, pp. 316–17.
12 *The Haydn String Quartet Society* (Hayes, Middlesex and London: The Gramophone Company), vol. 4 (1935), p. 9.
13 It was no doubt this type of technical self-consciousness that prompted the position taken to Haydn's art by Robert Sondheimer in his *Haydn: A Historical and Psychological Study Based on his Quartets* (London: Bernoulli, 1951). Op. 50 is discussed on pp. 117–27. For all the perversity of much of Sondheimer's argument, he does at least emphasize the obsessive side of Haydn's personality that is so much to the fore in Op. 50.

8 The individual works

1 *The Classical Style*, p. 123.
2 ('Six string quartets, Op. 50'), p. 5.
3 *Chronicle and Works*, vol. 2, p. 626.
4 Ibid.
5 'Gesture, form, and syntax in Haydn's music', in *Haydn Studies*, pp. 355–62.
6 See *The Classical Style*, pp. 120–5.
7 'Gesture, form, and syntax', "Discussion", p. 362. In an editorial note on p. 360, it is claimed that the traditional reading of the first violin part in bar 108 is corrupt and that it

should be as in bar 3. This would mean that the recapitulation begins melodically at bar 108 rather than 110, but, more startlingly, this 'correct' reading yields a whole bar of parallel fifths with the cello. No comment can be passed on this information until a critical report to an edition of Op. 50 has emerged.

8 ('Six string quartets, Op. 33'), notes to recording by the Tátrai Quartet (HCD 11887–88–2; 1979), trans. Charles F. Carlson, pp. 6–7.

9 See *Chronicle and Works*, vol. 3, pp. 199–200.

10 *The Great Haydn Quartets*, p. 90.

11 *Beyond Orpheus: Studies in Musical Structure* (Cambridge, Massachusetts: MIT Press, 1979), p. 78.

12 See *The Classical Style*, pp. 132–4.

13 As the lack of nicknames for the first four quartets of Op. 50 cannot have helped their cause in terms of frequency of performance, the present writer asked a seminar group to suggest names for the works. No. 2 was dubbed 'The High Jump Quartet' by Mr Robert Carey on account of the progressive raising of the interval 'jumped' by violin I in the minuet – from an octave in bars 0–1 to a ninth in bars 4–5, a minor tenth at 8–9, and a major tenth at 20–21, 'just like the bar for the high jump'.

14 *Sonata Forms* (New York: Norton, 1980), p. 161.

15 For an account of this aspect of the finale see Edward T. Cone, 'The uses of convention: Stravinsky and his models', *The Musical Quarterly* 48/3 (1962), pp. 287–99.

16 *Joseph Haydn and the String Quartet* (London: Barrie and Jenkins, 1974), p. 372.

17 *Haydn: His Life and Music*, p. 202.

18 'Franz Joseph Haydn', *Cyclopedic Survey of Chamber Music*, p. 543.

19 *The Great Haydn Quartets*, p. 99.

20 In *The String Quartet*, p. 53, Paul Griffiths notes the fact that there is no real recapitulatory answer to bars 38–42, 'the most extraordinary sound in the whole quartet'. However, at bars 81–2 of the slow movement the first violin plays an isolated fragment that represents a much-delayed motivic and registral response to the earlier passage. Given that this fragment (e^3 to a^3) occurs in a tonic A major context, it may be said to act as a resolution of its first-movement equivalent, thus providing further testimony to the long-range powers of Haydn's ear.

21 'Haydn's "Prussian" Quartets', p. 15.

22 Keller's term in *The Great Haydn Quartets*, p. 101.

23 *Haydn* (The Master Musicians), rev. edn (London: Dent, 1970), p. 163.

24 'Franz Joseph Haydn', *Cyclopedic Survey of Chamber Music*, p. 543.

25 *The Classical Style*, p. 138.

26 *The Great Haydn Quartets*, p. 103.

27 For a discussion of this process see Rosen, *The Classical Style*, p. 132.

28 See Georg Feder, 'Joseph Haydn 1982', in *Proceedings of the International Joseph Haydn Congress*, pp. 605–9.

29 *The Classical Style*, p. 129.

30 Whether or not Haydn consciously planned this specific connection, there can be little doubt that opening and closing the entire opus with works that open with a closing phrase was a deliberate large-scale pun.

31 *The Great Haydn Quartets*, p. 113.

32 *Poetics of Music* (New York: Harvard University Press, 1947), trans. Arthur Knodel and Ingolf Dahl, p. 68.

Select bibliography

Material specific to Op. 50

Barrett-Ayres, Reginald. *Joseph Haydn and the String Quartet*. London: Barrie and Jenkins, 1974

Blume, Friedrich. 'Joseph Haydns künstlerische Persönlichkeit in seinen Streich-quartetten'. In *Syntagma Musicologicum: Gesammelte Reden und Schriften*, ed. Martin Ruhnke. Kassel: Bärenreiter, 1963. Pp. 526–51

Geiringer, Karl. *Haydn: A Creative Life in Music*, 2nd edn, revised and enlarged in collaboration with Irene Geiringer. London: G. Allen and Unwin, 1964

Gray, Cecil. *The Haydn String Quartet Society*. Hayes, Middlesex and London: The Gramophone Company, vols. 4 (1935) and 7 [1938?]

Griffiths, Paul. *The String Quartet*. London: Thames and Hudson, 1983

Hughes, Rosemary. *Haydn* (The Master Musicians), rev. edn. London: Dent, 1970
Haydn String Quartets (BBC Music Guides). London: BBC Publications, 1966

Keller, Hans. *The Great Haydn Quartets: Their Interpretation*. London: Dent, 1986

Landon, H. C. Robbins. *Haydn: Chronicle and Works*, vol. 2: *Haydn at Esterháza 1766–1790*. London: Thames and Hudson, 1978
and Jones, David Wyn. *Haydn: His Life and Music*. London: Thames and Hudson, 1988

Larsen, Jens Peter, and Feder, Georg (work-list). 'Haydn, Franz Joseph'. *The New Grove Dictionary of Music and Musicians*, ed. Stanley Sadie. London: Macmillan, 1980. Vol. 8, pp. 328–407

Levy, Janet M. 'Gesture, form, and syntax in Haydn's music'. In *Haydn Studies: Proceedings of the International Haydn Conference, Washington, D.C., 1975*, ed. Jens Peter Larsen, Howard Serwer, and James Webster. New York-London: Norton, 1981. Pp. 355–62

Moe, Orin, Jr. 'The Implied Model in Classical Music'. *Current Musicology* No. 23 (1977), pp. 46–55
'The Significance of Haydn's Op. 33'. In *Haydn Studies*, pp. 445–50.

Rosen, Charles. *The Classical Style*. London: Faber and Faber, 1971
Sonata Forms. New York: Norton, 1980

Silbert, Doris. 'Ambiguity in the string quartets of Joseph Haydn'. *The Musical Quarterly* 36/4 (1950), pp. 562–73

Somfai, László. Untitled notes to recording of the Op. 50 quartets by the Tátrai Quartet, HCD 11934–35–2, 1987. Trans. Mária Steiner

Sondheimer, Robert. *Haydn: A Historical and Psychological Study Based on his Quartets.* London: Bernoulli, 1951

Thomas, Günter. 'Haydn's "Prussian" Quartets'. Notes to recording by the Tokyo String Quartet, DGG 423 509–2, 1976. Trans. John Coombs

Tovey, Donald Francis. 'Franz Joseph Haydn'. In *Cyclopedic Survey of Chamber Music,* comp. and ed. Walter Willson Cobbett. London: Oxford University Press, 1929. Vol. 1, pp. 514–48

General material

Adler, Guido. 'Haydn and the Viennese Classical School', trans. W. Oliver Strunk. *The Musical Quarterly* 18/2 (1932), pp. 191–207

Badura-Skoda, Eva. 'The Influence of the Viennese popular comedy on Haydn and Mozart'. *Proceedings of the Royal Musical Association* 100 (1974), pp. 185–99

Brendel, Alfred. 'A Mozart player gives himself advice', trans. Eugene Hartzell. *Gramophone,* March 1986, pp. 1133–4

Brown, A. Peter. 'Critical years for Haydn's instrumental music: 1787–90'. *The Musical Quarterly* 62/3 (1976), pp. 374–94

    Joseph Haydn's Keyboard Music: Sources and Style. Bloomington: Indiana University Press, 1986

    and Berkenstock, James T. 'Joseph Haydn in literature: a bibliography'. *Haydn-Studien* 3/3–4 (1974), pp. 173–352

Burke, Cornelius G. *The collector's Haydn,* with addendum by Arthur Cohn. Philadelphia: Lippincott, 1959

Clifton, Thomas. 'The poetics of musical silence'. *The Musical Quarterly* 62/2 (1976), pp. 163–81

Cone, Edward T. 'The uses of convention: Stravinsky and his models'. *The Musical Quarterly* 48/3 (1962), pp. 287–99

Gotwals, Vernon. *Joseph Haydn: Eighteenth Century Gentleman and Genius.* Madison: University of Wisconsin Press, 1963

Gruber, Gernot. 'Doppelgesichtiger Haydn?'. *Österreichische Musikzeitschrift* 37/3–4 (1982), pp. 139–46

Hodgson, Anthony. *The Music of Joseph Haydn: The Symphonies.* London: The Tantivy Press, 1976

Larsen, Jens Peter, Howard Serwer, and James Webster, eds. *Haydn Studies: Proceedings of the International Haydn Conference, Washington, D.C., 1975.* New York-London: Norton, 1981

LaRue, Jan. 'Multistage variance: Haydn's legacy to Beethoven'. *The Journal of Musicology* 1/3 (1982), pp. 265–74

Newman, William S. *The Sonata in the Classic Era.* Chapel Hill: University of North Carolina Press, 1963

Ratner, Leonard G. *Classic Music: Expression, Form, and Style.* New York: Schirmer, 1980

Rushton, Julian. *Classical Music: A Concise History from Gluck to Beethoven.* London: Thames and Hudson, 1986

Schroeder, David P. *Haydn and the Enlightenment: The Late Symphonies and their Audience.* Oxford: Clarendon Press, 1990

Sutcliffe, W. Dean. 'Haydn's Musical Personality'. *The Musical Times* 130/1756 (1989), pp. 341–4

Review of *The Great Haydn Quartets* by Hans Keller. *Music Analysis* 7/3 (1988), pp. 349–55

Walter, Horst. 'Haydn-Bibliographie 1973–1983'. *Haydn-Studien* 5/4 (1985), pp. 205–93

Index